The Gutsy Guide to Giving

In *The Gutsy Guide to Giving*, Elisabeth Williams shares her personal story of her journey to greater self-discovery with related advice about how self-awareness can lead to more insightful and strategic giving. This authentic and candid perspective is a joy to read for anyone who wants to connect their values with their philanthropy.

— Debra Mesch, PhD, Professor and Director, Women's Philanthropy Institute and Eileen Lamb O'Gara Chair in Women's Philanthropy, Indiana University Lilly Family School of Philanthropy

Lis Williams has written an inspiring book providing real life examples and offering challenges to jolt us out of our day-to-day routine. She summons us to use our gifts to make a positive impact every single day of our lives. *The Gutsy Guide to Giving* is a perfect gift for everyone you know!

— Lisa M. Dietlin, Author, Keynote Speaker, TV Personality, and President/CEO, Institute of Transformational Philanthropy

Elisabeth writes from her heart with the purpose of helping your heart access a deeper potential than you may have thought possible. If you take the journey she encourages you toward, you'll arrive at a place where you are both healed and freed to help others heal through your giving. Her words reflect a fundamental truth too often hidden in today's complex world with competing access to our dollars: Giving is about more than money. It's about how you live your best life while being connected to humanity. Generosity in this framework doesn't just change others, it changes us. You'll find in this book the tools and resources to consider your own authentic self and how that can translate into having a deep social impact in the world.

— Laura Zumdahl, PhD,
President and CEO, New Moms

Lis offers an important insight: To be whole and effective in all our relationships, we need to pay attention to and take care of our inner life. The mystery of the spiritual journey shows that care for our interior life provides access to our infinite beauty, and this always yields deep connection to others. Learning the skills to open the mind in the service of the heart is our calling, for our heart space is expansive and connected. Lis speaks of her travails and experiences as she searches for a way to fulfill her need to give and to connect, both in her immediate family and in the human family. She shows how the mind's projections of what it thinks is needed are too small, with results too few and burnout too common.

Lis's efforts to help us harness the awe we experience as we open ourselves to the flow of energy available to us in our soul's journey in this life are bound to be very helpful. My hope is that AWE Partners will contribute to the continuing evolution of human consciousness.

— Alan Krema, Chapter Coordinator,
Contemplative Outreach Chicago;
Graduate of the Center for Action and
Contemplation Living School; Facilitator,
Wisdom Way of Knowing Schools

The Gutsy Guide to Giving is exactly what every lady needs as a benchmark to explore her life's purpose. As women become more empowered, we take on roles that we never had to navigate before. This little gem of a book lays out, in the most awe-thentic form, how we already impact lives on a daily basis and can give more with authenticity. In the most heartfelt way, Elisabeth Williams not only held my hand but piggybacked me through analyzing life's tough questions. Bravo!

— Sheila Patel, Founder, LIFE Bags

If only I had this book to read fifteen years ago when my world fell apart. Not everyone has to uproot their life and move to another country to change their life as I did. All we have to do is uproot our inner lives to care for others—by far the most satisfying journey. People say uprooting my family to Africa to cofound mothers2mothers took courage. I say it was selfish. Lis calls it a heroic journey to life's purpose; I call it the only way to really live. And opening the pages of this book is a great place to start!

— Robin A Smalley, Cofounder
and Chief Connector, Mothers2Mothers

Lis Williams does a great job illustrating how we must do the important work of healing ourselves in order to do the equally important work of healing this world. *The Gutsy Guide to Giving* is a fantastic resource for those who want to use their gifts to make a lasting and profound difference in the lives of others.

— John Stracks, MD

Lis Williams' words brilliantly ignite readers to lead a life of soul-fulfilling purpose. *The Gutsy Guide to Giving* is a golden ticket that every woman not only has the right but the gifts to cash in. She gives readers the tools and inspiration to make an extraordinary impact on the issues that live deep within their hearts. Expect freedom and fulfillment to fuel you as you follow Lis' one-of-a-kind guidance.

— Maegan Watson, Founder, Watson Style Group

Elisabeth Williams' journey is inspiring and relatable, and it lends approachable encouragement to those who are looking for guidance in paving their way into the philanthropic space, regardless of income or network. *The Gutsy Guide to Giving* inspires us to create awe-thentic impact.

— Liz Dozier, Managing Director, Chicago Beyond

Joyce~
Be AWE-dacious!
Love You,
Lisbeth

The Gutsy Guide to Giving

YOUR JOURNEY TO AWE-THENTIC IMPACT

Elisabeth A. Williams

The Gutsy Guide to Giving: Your Journey to Awe-thentic Impact
Elisabeth A. Williams

Copyright 2018 by Elisabeth A. Williams

All rights reserved. No part of this book, in part or in whole, may be reproduced in any written, electronic, recording, or photocopy form without the prior written permission of the publisher except for the inclusion of brief quotations in a review.

AWE Partners, LLC
www.AWEPartners.com

ISBN: 978-0-9994047-1-3
E-Book ISBN: 978-0-9994047-0-6
LCCN: 2017954202

Editing by Melanie Mulhall, Dragonheart
Cover Design by Step Brightly
Interior Design by Nick Zelinger, NZ Graphics

First Edition
Published in the United States of America

Contents

Introduction 13
1. Happy and Human 21
2. Where Are You Stuck?............................ 25
3. You Are Good Enough........................... 28
4. Make Space for Grace 36
5. Nurture Your Soul 40
6. Take Care of You 44
7. Live Life with More Awe 48
8. Your Magnificence and Your Calling 54
9. Face Your Fears and Shine Your Light............. 61
10. Piercing the Dark................................ 67
11. Learning to Fly 72
12. The Art and Soul of Giving....................... 78
13. Reality Check.................................... 81
14. The Overhead Myth and Impact Measurement 85
15. Effective Altruism 94
16. Portfolio of Giving............................... 98

17. Social Enterprises and Impact Investing.	105
18. Just Begin.	111
Appendix A: Tips from the Giving Guru	115
Appendix B: To Give or Not to Give	120
Appendix C: Causes and Issues	129
Appendix D: The Awe-thentic Approach to Identifying Effective Organizations	131
Appendix E: Gutsy Guidebook	137
Appendix F: Portfolio of Giving	154
Acknowledgments	157
About the Author	161

Just Be

You are a human being,
So how much being are you doing?
If all you are doing is doing,
Then your doing is not as it should be.
Your doing is running,
Your doing is hiding,
Your doing is proving,
Your doing is striving,
Your doing is achieving,
Your doing is fighting.
Your doing is not you.
You are you.
Just be.
Be still,
Be quiet,
Be empty,
Be open,
Be you,
Be whole,
Be fearless,
Be free.
Just be.

— Elisabeth A. Williams

Introduction

My first experience of volunteering was traumatic. I was a candy striper at a rehab center near our home and probably in fifth or sixth grade. Once a week, my girlfriends and I donned our red-striped aprons and hats and headed out. Our duties typically consisted of feeding individuals who were severely disabled. Their bodies were contorted and they couldn't communicate. I was particularly troubled by a couple of the residents: a woman in her forties with multiple sclerosis and a teenaged boy who had sustained a neck injury in a high school football game. Both were surrounded by the elderly and infirm, and they seemed completely out of place. I am amazed that I stuck with it so long because I never looked forward to going to that rehab center.

I learned then that my gift was not in the medical field. I couldn't stomach it. I had nightmares anytime I watched a TV show that had anything to do with illness or injury.

But I also learned that I was extremely blessed and that when I shared myself with those in need, I felt an incredible sense of fulfillment. This was the beginning of a lifetime of service. It was also the beginning of an important understanding: we all have different gifts and we are all called to serve in different ways.

In college, I became a "big sister" to a young girl from a poor neighborhood near my university. I would ride my bike to her home, where we shared the kitchen counter space with roaches as we baked cookies. She would get dressed up on a Friday night and sleep over at my sorority house. We loved being together, and I was learning that I could make a difference by just being me and doing the things I enjoyed.

I continued volunteering with a tutoring program once I graduated. Fourth Presbyterian Church in Chicago had a cadre of volunteers who worked one-on-one with children from the Cabrini Green housing projects. My little girl and I spent time on her schoolwork, but every once in a while, we took a field trip. One night I took her up to the top of the John Hancock building. She got out of the elevator, looked out the window, and exclaimed, "Wow! Is this the world?"

No, this is just a small piece of the world, I thought. Sadly, I knew it might be the only piece of the larger world she would ever see because despite my attempts to widen her vision, the odds were stacked against her.

At that time, I was working in the corporate world and feeling utterly unfulfilled. Although I liked working with numbers and people, I loathed the bureaucracy and lack of autonomy. So while pursuing my MBA at night, I decided to expand my studies beyond finance into the fields of entrepreneurship and nonprofit organization management. That's when things began to change. I got a taste of what my life could be like if I were to make a career shift. It was the first step on a path that has been anything but straight, yet always an adventure.

During that same time period, I met the love of my life, Jack. We married, started a family, and eventually moved to Charlotte, North Carolina. Following a tremendous amount of angst and soul searching, I chose to put my career on hold to become a stay-at-home mom. It was a heart-wrenching decision but one I have never regretted.

Ten years later, I was sitting in my home office in Charlotte, North Carolina, sifting through files in anticipation of our move back to Chicago, when I came across a folder filled with research on the state of children in the inner cities. I had collected that information years before when I was creating the Summit Tutoring Program, a partnership between our parish, St. Michael's, and Blessed Sacrament Youth Center in the North Lawndale community on the west side of Chicago.

As I sat on the floor reading from that file, what struck me was that nothing had changed. In the fifteen years since the tutoring program began, nothing had changed for our children in the inner cities. Things were at least as bad as they had been. Arguably, they were worse. And I wondered to myself how I would feel if I had spent the last fifteen years running that tutoring program only to question whether my efforts had been for naught.

Since those first days at the rehab center, I have volunteered, sat on boards, worked for a nonprofit and a social enterprise, consulted to the nonprofit community, and created programs for schools and churches. I have met people who are profoundly dedicated to their organizations and their missions and whose lives are a testament to self-sacrifice and compassion. But I have also been frustrated by the slow pace of progress in solving our most entrenched societal ills, and I have made it my life's work to determine how we can solve those problems more effectively.

The world often seems to be in chaos. And whether it is the larger world or some smaller piece of it like our nation or our community, bad news is what we usually hear and read in the media. It is easy to feel paralyzed and do nothing about it. We're busy, often in survival mode, just trying to make it through, day by day. We can't take on another thing, but somehow, that just doesn't feel right.

We don't want to be so wrapped up in our own lives that we do nothing for others whose lives are falling apart, so we write a check to an organization that advertises on TV, attend a fundraising event for a cause that a friend supports, or join our faith community in collecting food, clothes, and household items to donate to a local shelter. And then we go back to our ordinary life. When the next disaster strikes, we feel that nudge again to do more, if we only knew how.

We want to fix things, make them better. We want to fix other people and the world so we don't have to worry or feel guilty. But is the discomfort only with the world outside, or does it also reside within? What if the path to effective giving doesn't start out there? What if the path starts within—within you, with your soul?

The heroine's journey to awe-thentic impact begins with you. It takes you inward first so you can be more effective on the outside. You heal yourself so you can light the dark and heal the world. But don't be fooled. The inward journey is not an easier journey than the outward one. It is also not any less scary.

So why would you want to go there? Well, sister, the truth is, you're already there. You're already on the heroine's journey. You just may not know it because, God knows, your life may not look like a romantic tale and you may not feel like a heroine. In fact, you may feel like a damsel in distress most days, wondering where in the hell your knight in shining armor is and how all those kids got there. I know because I've been there too. But trust me, there is a heroine's journey wrapped up inside your messy, chaotic, overwhelming life. And all this is leading you to your highest good.

The Gutsy Guide to Giving is just that, a guide. It's a process you can use to look deeply at your life and find the courage to heal the broken places, uncover your unique gifts, identify the causes that cry out to you, determine where and how you want to share yourself, and know that you are doing your part to make an impact in the world. You can move at your own pace. Work from start to finish or just focus on the chapters that draw you in and the areas of your life where you desire clarity. Take a week, a month, a year, or a decade.

Like just about everything else in life, the journey toward effective giving is not a straight line. The places within you that need healing not only impact your quality of life, they impact how you see the world. And that cannot help but impact your desire to give back to the world and the ways in which you contribute when you do give. If you lack self-confidence and self-worth, you may play small, and that affects what and how you give back to the world. If you give all of your time and energy to others without taking care of yourself, your internal well will be dry. And yes, you will eventually have nothing to offer others.

On the other hand, if you develop self-confidence and self-worth, you'll have clearer internal sight for seeing the beauty in others. Your own wounds do not cloud things. If you take care of yourself, you will develop inner peace, which then flows out from you to behavior that creates and inspires peace in the world. You will have compassion for yourself, allowing you to have compassion for others.

Self-exploration impacts who you are, how you see the world, and how you move through the world. And that has a profound impact on your giving. In turn, your giving leads you back to self-exploration. Visualize a spiral that moves upwards as you continue to journey inward and take the learning, healing, and growth outward into the world.

Because who we are is deeply connected to how we think about giving, I am going to begin by exploring the perfection in our imperfection, the places where we get stuck, and the need for self-care and soul-care. And I'm going to share a bit of my own journey in the process—not because I believe my life has been so fascinating and is worthy of a memoir but because I hope in reading about my journey, you will see something of yourself. After all, our stories are different, but our journey is the same.

I hope you'll explore this journey with me, the heroine's journey to your life's purpose, deeper meaning, and awethentic impact. It takes courage. It takes grit. It takes guts. But you're up to the challenge. You've been preparing all your life. Begin by putting your foot on the path. Don't worry. I promise to be right there with you.

1

Happy and Human

I love starting a new year. I love the freshness of it, of leaving the old behind and getting out my new calendar with all of the white space just waiting to be filled in. I love setting new goals and figuring out how I'm going to get there. I love the mystery of what lies ahead and the hope inherent in a year that is happy and new.

If only it was that easy. If only we could just chart our course, make our year happy and new, and make our dreams come true—or even better, make our life happy and new, not just this year but every year.

In my younger years, I typically felt pretty happy most days. But as time went on, life became more challenging. It finally got to the point where I often didn't feel new or happy. I felt tired, weighed down, and pessimistic. If my genes were anything like my ancestors, I was going to be around for a very long time. I didn't want to spend another fifty or sixty years feeling weary and negative, so I committed to doing whatever it took to rediscover happy and new in the form of peace, joy, and abundance. That was what I really wanted, and that was how I wanted to live.

What about you? Is life turning out the way you planned? Is it everything you thought it would be? Have your dreams come true? If your life is fulfilling your dreams, then rock on, sister! If not, then what are you going to do about it? You *can* do something about it, and if that is what you want to do, then this is a place where you can begin to rediscover who you really are and what you have to share with the world. You can find meaning and reconnect with your soul, your passions, and your power.

If you're looking for a quick fix or just want to know which charity to donate to, this is not the place for you. But if you are ready to make peace with the past, awaken the new, and embrace life more fully, then welcome to the awe-thentic impact journey!

If you are ripe for this journey, then know that I'm ready to serve as your personal Sherpa. But before I do, I need to come clean with you: I'm not perfect. There, I said it! I'm also not Superwoman. I can't do it all. How do I know? I know because I've tried and failed. I've made mistakes and fallen flat on my face. I've sinned and been wounded. And just so you know, I haven't done those things for the last time. I will keep doing them.

Yet here I am, alive and breathing, upright and striving, taking epic chances and pursuing bold dreams. I'm strong, courageous, and passionate. You are too! I already know this about you because just the fact that you are here with me tells me that you are looking for a better way to live and a better way to give—not just for you, but also for your family and friends, your community, and the world.

Here's the thing, though, and whether or not you want to hear it, I have to be honest. In fact, I promise to be honest with you always because I care about you. If you want to get to peace, joy, and abundance, if you want your dreams to come true, and if you want to live life more fully, you're going to have to do your work. I'm not talking about your job here. I'm talking about your inner work, the work of the soul. It's the kind of work that requires you to lay down your shield, take off your armor, and stand naked in front of the mirror just staring at your reflection.

When you start to do the work, you start asking the serious questions of life: Who am I? Who the hell am I? If I'm not just a daughter, sister, wife, mother, friend, employee, volunteer, triathlete, rock star, and rocket scientist, then who am I really? And what is stopping me from being all that I can possibly be? What wound, or sin, or failure, or excuse, or regret, or fear am I hanging onto? And why on earth won't I let it go?

If you're still holding on, it's time to work through it and let it go, dear sister. Why? Because if you want to be at your best, if you want to pursue your calling, if you want to light the dark and heal the world, you must first heal yourself. I know it's scary. I know it's a lot easier to go about life the way you have been. I know it's easier to stay busy because then you don't have to feel.

But I can tell you that there's no better feeling than the feeling of freedom that accompanies releasing the past, embracing your truth, and becoming all that God created you to be. I will be waiting for you right here when you're ready to move on. You have to do this in your own time. But please don't put it off much longer. Life is waiting for you, and the world needs your unique gifts and talents, your love and compassion, your strength and your beauty.

What are you waiting for?

2

Where Are You Stuck?

Do you ever feel stuck, like you want to move but can't, like you're holding on to something or something is holding on to you and you can't break free? We all become stuck sometimes—in the messiness of the world, in the responsibilities of life, and in our own brokenness.

So where does it show up and how do we get unstuck? The most obvious ways we feel stuck seem external. You might feel stuck in a dead-end job or a difficult marriage. You might feel stuck at home caring for small children or elderly parents. Whatever your circumstances, these places where you feel stuck are real, and it may be time to figure out just how to make the situation you are in better.

Another way to explore your stuck places is to look inside yourself. You can get stuck in poor choices and bad habits. You might not like to talk about these things because doing so can make you feel vulnerable and defensive. Depending on how you were raised, it can even make you feel terrible about yourself. Because of that, you may prefer to avoid going there.

Some people struggle with feelings of jealousy or pride and find that they are judgmental or prone to gossip. Others have a tendency to lie, cheat, or steal. But to get unstuck, you're going to have to face the truth. We all make mistakes, but that doesn't make us unlovable.

One obstinate place many of us find ourselves stuck is in our woundedness. Some of us grew up under really difficult circumstances, and the wounds we carry are gaping holes in our hearts that we think will never heal. Others have not faced profoundly traumatic experiences, but just growing up and making our way in the world can leave us wounded and battle-scarred. Wounds can show up as guilt, shame, or resentment. They can manifest themselves through anger or even rage. They can be seen in our fear, worry, anxiety, and depression.

It is really difficult to face the pain of our woundedness. So we push it down, bury it, and focus on things that are more positive. But we can only run for so long. At some point in our lives, usually by midlife if not before, things begin to surface, and we realize that we just can't fake it anymore.

But here's the good news. It's okay. It's all okay. You don't need to hide anymore. You don't need to pretend. Despite your mistakes and wounds, you are good and you are loved—

unconditionally. No matter where you struggle or where your wounds are, forgiveness and acceptance are always available.

And here's the deal. The places where we are broken, the places where we are stuck, have a dramatic impact on our quality of life. They keep us in bondage and mire us in guilt, shame, anger, resentment, and fear. The result is that we are immersed in negative energy, and it is that negative energy that we take out into the world. When we look at the world through a negative lens, it is difficult to give from a place other than our own woundedness. That may express itself through misguided attempts to save others while ignoring the need to save ourselves. It may express itself through resentment towards those in need. It may express itself in judgment or pity toward those you serve. But it will not express itself through effective, joyful giving. To be gutsy givers, we first must get ourselves unstuck.

The journey that you are embarking on can be scary, and it takes great courage to make this journey. But you are brave, and you are not alone. When you're tempted to turn around and go back to your old ways, don't. Just keep moving forward one step at a time. I promise you that it will be worth it. God is just waiting to shower your life with peace, joy, and abundance.

3

You Are Good Enough

───────•───────

Not so long ago, I had one of those experiences of knowing I was being taught a very important lesson by life. But that knowledge did not stop the pain from being excruciating. It all began when my husband and I took our youngest son to an appointment with a college counselor. In two short years I will be sending my second and last child off to college, which is sure to bring out a whole host of other life lessons.

What was supposed to be a first step in the long road to college acceptance triggered something I had no idea was hiding out in me. Our conversation centered around who my son was and what he was looking for in a college. We discussed his academic credentials and his desire to play soccer. We talked about the size of the school he would like to attend, the geographic locations he preferred, and what he thought he'd like to study.

Then the counselor asked my son about his extracurricular activities. She told him that he would need to begin creating his activity list and printed out a copy of one that a former client had prepared. The implication was that without an impeccable activity list, his chance of getting into an elite institution was questionable, despite his stellar academic record and the fact that he just happens to be a terrific kid. (Yes, that's his mother talking, but it's true, dammit!) We finished our discussion and parted ways.

On the car ride home, I began pondering the fact that the playing field is not level. It's not fair that every child can't afford to hire a college counselor whose job it is to do everything they can to get that child into the best possible school. It's not fair that every child can't hire a writer to edit their college essays. It's not fair that every child can't afford to hire a tutor to help them prepare for their college entrance exams or get a better grade in their litany of AP classes that, apparently, they shouldn't be in anyway if they need a tutor! Is it just me or is that insanity?

Life's not fair! But we already knew that.

Then I glanced at the activity list the counselor had printed out and gasped. This so-called teenager had accomplished more in his four years of high school than most people accomplish in a lifetime of careers. Before turning eighteen, this prodigy was the vice president of one of the top math teams in the state. Each week, for fun, they reviewed conic sections, trigonometric functions, Cartesian geometry, polynomials and roots, and combinatorics. He was the president of his school's physics, engineering, and technology club, which was working on remotely operated vehicles. He was a math tutor. He had taken a college course at Northwestern and had attended a summer camp on number theory at Stanford, and he had studied black holes and quantum mechanics at Brown. I wondered why the hell he was going to college because it seemed to me that he already had the equivalent of a college education.

My first thought was that someone had permitted this young boy to miss his childhood. They had encouraged him to do everything "right" so he could get into the best educational institution in the country. They thought that would make him happy and successful in life, so they had pushed him to grow up quickly, thus providing him an edge in a race to nowhere. And sadly, he had obeyed.

Mind you, I did not know if any of these things were true. It could be said that they were the hallucinations rumbling around in my head in response to that activity sheet.

But it was the second thought that led to my awakening. It began when I started to question myself and continued with that questioning for days. Why hadn't I encouraged my son to stick with math club, even though he found it boring? Why hadn't I signed him up for engineering camp instead of a leadership conference? Might he have done research with a professor some summer instead of playing soccer? I hadn't researched it. In fact, why had I let him play soccer or anything else outdoors when he was little instead of studying advanced science and math indoors?

But it didn't stop there. No, I went on to question every decision I had ever made about my older son who was already at the "wrong" college. Why did I not force my brilliant, rebellious son to get the grades he was capable of in high school, even though he was bored and loathed studying? Why didn't I insist that he fully annotate the novel *Cat's Eye*, even though it's a book that only women in midlife would enjoy? Why didn't I let him continue to participate in Model UN, a club that looks great on a college application, despite the fact that the weekend conferences were "supervised" by college students and the kids were drinking and smoking pot? Why on earth did I think that a college focused on growing the mind, body, spirit, and emotions would serve him well in life?

And what about earlier in his life? Why hadn't I insisted that he stay in Boy Scouts so he could earn the coveted rank of Eagle Scout even though the only activity he enjoyed was spelunking? Why hadn't I breast-fed longer? Why hadn't I played more classical music to my growing fetus? Why hadn't I gotten pregnant when I was younger and my cells were more robust? Why, why, why?

Not long after that visit with the college counselor, I began having back pain. Being very in tune with the mind-body connection, I knew my body was sending me a message. I just wasn't sure what it was.

As fate would have it, the spirituality center near my home was holding a retreat on the Sedona Method, which teaches that a sense of lack and our desire for control, security, and approval give rise to our emotions. Those desires make us feel insecure because we believe we are lacking something we need to feel complete. The balm that heals is loving, unconditional presence. Was it possible that my endless self-questioning following that meeting stemmed from a sense of lack? Did I feel I lacked the ability to control what was happening with my sons? Did I feel insecure about my children's futures and my ability to make decisions that would impact their futures in a positive way? Was I seeking the approval of my peers and the larger world based on what college my boys attended?

I had to admit that the answer was yes to all of those questions. It was a breakthrough. I eased up on myself and the back pain lessened.

But three days later, I was writhing in pain on my family room floor. Perhaps I didn't have it all figured out after all. Three Advil capsules, along with some heat and stretching, and I was able to sit upright enough to try working through the emotions. What was I resisting? What wall was blocking my ability to move forward? As I thought more about it, I realized that it was not a wall but a ceiling—my inner glass ceiling. That ceiling had been hanging over my head for a long time, and there were words etched in the glass: you're not good enough.

It was a stunning realization. I had not seen myself as a person who thought she wasn't good enough, and I could not imagine anyone ever telling me that when I was growing up. But then I began thinking about it. One time in elementary school, I wasn't invited to a party. In seventh grade, I was cut from the cheerleading squad, and in eighth grade, my friends decided to room with someone else during a trip to Washington, DC. I ran for class secretary once and lost, and more than once, I liked a boy who didn't like me back. I got a D on an assignment. A boyfriend broke up with me. I dropped a college class because I was failing it. I applied for a job I didn't get and started a business that didn't get off the ground. The mistakes I feared I'd made parenting had plenty of company for what I might have subconsciously thought were my failures in life.

Were these all examples of not being good enough? At some level within me, they apparently were. They were just normal, everyday experiences of growing up and growing out into the world, but at some level, they had stung badly enough that I had internalized them as evidence I wasn't good enough. Buried deep within my psyche, that feeling had created a glass ceiling.

I knew I wasn't alone in this. Those interior thoughts and feelings create walls, ceilings, and entire houses that keep us trapped. By our own making, we are kept in our place—our nice, safe place. There is, of course, a problem with it. It may feel comfortable some of the time, but it is actually a small, tight space. It's hard to breathe in there. It's hard to move freely.

That cramped space restrains us until we have had enough and refuse to let it contain us anymore. When the life force inside us that has always been there begins to bubble, churn, and push its way out of the depths of the soul, the truth of who we are emerges.

Sometimes that happens in a fit of unbearable back pain; sometimes it happens in even more uncomfortable ways.

Now here's the truth: You are good enough. You always have been good enough. You always will be good enough. You don't have to change. You don't have to do or be anything to be good enough. You already are.

Not only are you good enough, you are magnificent! You are brilliant, beautiful, gifted, talented, and beloved. You are a daughter of the king, which makes you a princess.

And so am I.

How do I know these things? I know them because when we explore ourselves in depth, when we peel away everything that is not authentically us, what is left is the true, authentic self. And that is not only good enough, it is a wondrous thing.

When we don't know that we're good enough, right down to the level of our DNA, we play small. And we don't think we could possibly be enough to have something to give to others. If we actually do make little forays into the world of sharing our gifts, we don't show up fully. We don't take the risks necessary to make lasting change. We don't shine our light.

But we *are* good enough. And together we just might light the world on fire.

Anyone have a match?

4

Make Space for Grace

———•———

There's a space between the chapters of our lives that can be difficult to accept. It's a transition time. Some refer to it as liminal space. It's when you know what has been is ending but you are not yet sure what is to come.

Sometimes we're happy to have a chapter in our life close, especially if it's been a challenging or frustrating one. At other times, it's not so easy to let go of what was, particularly if we can't see what's up ahead. The reality is that transitions are an inevitable part of life. Circumstances are always changing. Nothing stays the same.

So what do we do with this? How do we navigate those liminal times in our lives in a way that is healthy, hopeful, and open to growth? To do this, we have to immerse ourselves fully in the place of uncertainty. We have to feel it completely—the sorrow, the fear, the anticipation, and the hope—and we have to make space for grace.

When my oldest son left for college, I knew it was coming. He made it through four years of high school, took all the college tests, filled out the applications, selected his roommates, and got his housing squared away. He was so ready. He couldn't wait to get out of high school, move out of the house, leave our tiny community, and venture into the great unknown.

I was ready too. The high school years had been challenging, and I'd had enough of it. I was ready for him to be in a new environment, test his wings, and grow into the remarkable man I knew he had the potential to be. Yet despite all the joy at what the future held for him, there was an incredible aching for what we were all leaving behind.

For nineteen years, he had rarely slept a night away from us. Other than a few overnight camp trips, we had always been together. We ate meals together and talked almost every day. I'd seen his face and been able to touch him, so I'd known that he was okay. But all of that changed, and I knew that change was permanent. It was unlikely that he would live under my roof again for any length of time. Our lives would never again be as entwined as they had been for the first nineteen years of his life. And I knew that this was all unfolding the way it was meant to. I got it.

But knowing all those things did not make it any easier. It still hurt like hell to let him go.

When he came home for the first time at Thanksgiving, it had been eight weeks since he'd left for college. I looked in his bedroom and saw his suitcase. His toiletry kit was in the bathroom. It hit me then that he was a visitor. His life was elsewhere, and he was just visiting.

Wherever his dad and I live will always be home to him, at a profound level. But he will eventually create his own home, and ours will be a place he visits.

Around the time he was leaving for college, there were a lot of Facebook posts about kids heading off to school and the sorrow felt by their mothers. One woman commented in a way that put it all in perspective for me. "Send your son off to war and then tell me how hard it is to watch him leave," she said.

I could not fathom how overwhelmingly difficult that would be, and I felt for the women who watched their children go off to war. I could only imagine that it would be utterly heartbreaking. My initial response after seeing her comment was to stop feeling sorry for myself and get over it. It could be so much worse. But the truth was that my initial response was not a healthy one. It was very familiar, something I had done a lot in the past, but that did not make it a healthy response. I had a history of pretending everything was okay and avoiding my feelings. Of course, the problem is that your feelings don't go away just because you do your best to avoid them. They just get stuck in your body, and eventually, they have to come out. They may come out through fits of tears, through anger, through physical pain, or through illness. But they will come out.

The answer isn't to suck it up. The answer isn't to count your blessings and move on. As my bestie, Donna, says, "Sometimes you gotta stick with the ick."

We have to feel our feelings, even—and especially—the hard ones. We have to feel them all the way through so we can incorporate them into our being. We need to learn what they have to teach us about ourselves and about life. We have to let them make us human so we can experience the divine.

Transitions are uncomfortable, but until we extricate the old from our lives, we do not have the internal space and freedom to invite in the new. The space between life chapters is sacred space. It's where earth and heaven meet. It is where we come to know ourselves and discover the deeper meaning and purpose of our life. When we accept the space between the chapters, we are inviting divine magic to come into play. We are making space for grace.

Stay there long enough to glimpse the beauty and wonder of what was and what is to come.

5

Nurture Your Soul

———————•———————

The French theologian and scientist Pierre Teilhard de Chardin said, "We are not human beings having a spiritual experience. We are spiritual beings having a human experience." Take a moment and really think about that. What does it mean to be a spiritual being having a human experience? Does it make you think about your life differently? Does it make you wonder if you are living the way you are meant to live? And if we are spiritual beings having a human experience, what are you, as a human, doing to care for your spirit? Questions like these have the potential to change everything.

For most of my life I was a doer with a capital D. I prided myself on how much I could accomplish. I loved having a to-do list, and I loved, loved, loved checking things off my list. I was the queen of multitasking, and I thought the way I was living my life was exactly the way life was meant to be lived.

Having children changed everything for me. I could no longer make out my list of things to do and be sure everything would be checked off by the end of the day. The precious beings that had taken over my life did not appear to have a clue about how important my list was to my sense of self-worth. They constantly interrupted me with requests for food, shelter, and clothing. They demanded love and attention as well as clean diapers, kisses for boo-boo's, and a daily dose of hugs, giggles, and pure fun. It took me years to surrender to the fact that my list might need to wait.

These same adorable children brought me face-to-face with my fears. The thought of anything bad happening to them was overwhelming. And as the chaos of the world swirled around me, I knew I had to find a place that felt safe. So I began to pursue my spirituality more fully. Praying was something I had done since I was a child, so I started talking with God more frequently. I had a lot to say and a lot of requests to make. But I rarely made time to stop and listen.

As I continued on my journey, the idea of meditating kept showing up. Ideally, I was supposed to meditate twice a day for twenty minutes at a time. Two things came to mind: How on earth would I ever find time? And wasn't it boring? As a lifelong doer, I just could not imagine what good could possibly come from sitting still for twenty minutes and trying not to think about anything.

But curiosity got the better of me, so each morning after the kids left for school and I had my breakfast, I ascended to the third floor of my home and camped out on the overstuffed chair where I used to read to my children. I had read that you are supposed to sit up straight with your feet on the floor, but I'm a bit of a rebel, so I did it my way.

Now I cannot imagine beginning my day without meditating. And when I actually began to listen to God instead of just talking to him, it changed my life. Slowing down and becoming a be-er as well as a doer has also changed my life. Taking care of my soul has transformed me in ways that I never could have imagined.

Some mystics teach that the human soul comes from God and that the last thing God does before putting a soul into the body is kiss it. If you haven't felt that kiss in a long time, I want that for you. We are spiritual beings having a human experience. And to be most fully alive, we must nurture our soul. We must rediscover our true self. We must rest in God.

Contemplation is this resting in God. Get there by any means you can: prayer, meditation, reading spiritual material, journaling, attending a worship service, spending time in nature, viewing or making art, listening to or making music, dancing—whatever. But get there!

To light the dark and heal the world you must ignite the flame within you and share that light with those whose light has dimmed or been extinguished altogether. To make an authentic impact in the world you must align with your Source so that you can receive the guidance to know your path and find the courage to follow it.

Take time to nurture your soul!

6

Take Care of You

———————•———————

In the Judeo-Christian tradition, the first commandment is "Love your God with all your heart and with all your soul and with all your mind." The second commandment is "Love your neighbor as yourself." It's this second commandment that I find intriguing.

If the second commandment is to love your neighbor *as yourself*, then I would submit to you that if you ain't doin' a good job lovin' on yourself, there ain't no way you're doin' a good job lovin' on others. Let's explore this.

There is a longtime belief in some quarters that God should come first, others should come second, and you should come third. When I was young and naïve, I decided that this was a way of being that I should adopt. Now that I'm older and somewhat wiser, I understand that this is absolutely *not* the way to live. It is, in fact, the quickest way to ensure that you end up burnt out, angry, and resentful.

I was raised to be a good girl. Among other things, that meant that I should do what I was told, clean up my messes, color within the lines, and take care of those in need. So like any good little girl, I developed what I call a Savior of the World Complex. If I didn't take care of it, who would? If I didn't "fix" people, they might continue to live their lives in utter hell. If I didn't discover the cure for cancer, end world hunger, and lead the world to peace, once and for all, then these things just would not get done. Surely, no one else could possibly take care of these things as well as me. It was as if I were carrying a backpack, and whenever I came across someone in need, I would ask if I could carry a bit of their burden. Most were happy to hand it over, so I put it in my backpack and carried on.

As you can imagine, the backpack became heavier and heavier over time. I began to experience chronic neck and shoulder pain. This lasted for years until I finally got sick and tired of the pain and was determined to find a way to relieve it. That took me on a journey that led to my discovering the link between emotions and physical well-being. I began seeing a physician who specialized in integrative medicine, and that physician suggested I work through a book by Dr. Howard Schubiner titled *Unlearn Your Pain.*

One of the most healing practices offered in that book was the encouragement to write—but not send—letters to people in your life. And because they would not be sent, they could be letters to those who were dead as well as those who were alive. The theory was that our physical pain can be caused by unexpressed rage and that by writing about it, we can release it. I was skeptical because I didn't feel any rage. Maybe a little anger here and there, but good girls don't feel rage.

Despite my skepticism, I began writing. And lo and behold, the rage just spilled onto the page as if I were vomiting up years of emotion held captive. I was stunned. And there wasn't just rage. There was grief, guilt, and fear in there as well, all just stuck inside waiting to be released so I could be set free.

Once the emotional and physical turmoil began to subside, I could begin to see things from a newer, healthier perspective. I realized that by putting everyone and everything before myself, I was worn out, angry, and lost. I couldn't even remember who I was. Not only was I hurting myself by putting everyone's needs before my own, but in playing savior, I actually disempowered people by teaching them to rely on me instead of relying on themselves and God. Sometimes the best gift you can give someone is to let them discover just how powerful they are.

The best givers also know how to receive, so it is important to find a healthy balance between giving and receiving. I began practicing more self-care to balance my tendency to give myself away to others. Here's what self-care looks like to me: taking time for my spiritual practices; working through difficult emotions; sleeping well; eating healthily; exercising in ways that I love; taking baths; learning how to say no without feeling guilty; staying away from toxic people and situations; pursuing my calling; laughing more; and having fun.

If you are always putting others first, I urge you to consider a new way of living. You need to be healthy and whole to make your awe-thentic impact in the world. Take care of you!

7

Live Life with More Awe

As my children got older and I had more free time, I decided to reinvent myself. One of the things I really wanted was to live with more awe. For quite some time, I had felt restless, as if something were missing. I had a wonderful marriage and two great kids. My needs were met, as well as many of my wants. My restlessness just didn't make a lot of sense to me.

Something within me felt that there was a deeper, more magical way of living, and I wanted to experience that. Every so often, I read about or met someone who seemed to be living that way, so I knew it was possible. But I wasn't sure how to get there.

About that time, I read what would become one of my favorite books, *A Million Miles in a Thousand Years* by Donald Miller. After writing a best-selling memoir, Miller had been approached by producers to make a film about his life. That made him rethink the story of his life, and he began questioning just how meaningful it was.

I started to wonder whose story I was living. Was this the story that God intended for my life when he knit me in my mother's womb? Was I writing my own story or living one written and directed by my family, my upbringing, my education, and society? To be honest, I felt like I was playing small, like I was told I could only go so far but no further and had believed it.

And then, of course, there were the fears. (I'm a six on the Enneagram, so fear comes naturally to me.) There was always so much to be afraid of. And stepping out into life more fully was sure to invite challenges, struggles, and heartache. Who needs more of that?

Isn't it easier to hunker down, stay in your safe cocoon, and bide your time until it's over? But let's be honest. That's not living! That's existing. And I wanted more out of life. So I started to wonder why one of the most frequently appearing phrases in the Bible is one version or another of be not afraid. Could there be something to that? Is it possible to stop living in fear and begin living with faith? Was it possible that life wasn't meant to be scary, that we weren't supposed to suffer so much? Could we actually live in peace, joy, and abundance instead of fear? If so, I wanted in.

Recognizing that this would take some work, I began reading books like *Wired for Joy* and *The Chemistry of Calm*. I learned that we can actually rewire our brains away from fear and toward joy. I started listening to Hay House CDs, podcasts, and radio shows by authors and speakers who seemed to be living more positively, like Wayne Dyer and Dr. Christiane Northrup. I began watching Oprah Winfrey's show, *Super Soul Sunday*.

And slowly, things began to change. I felt calmer and didn't worry so much. I stopped thinking about all of the things I could be afraid of and started thinking about all of the things I wanted to do with my life.

I stopped asking, "What if . . . ?" and started saying, "What if . . . !" And I wrote down a long list of what my life would look like if it were magical. Here are just a few of the things I wrote: I wouldn't be afraid. I would let go and let God. I would embrace the guidance and power of the Holy Spirit. I would be grateful for all of my blessings. I would surround myself with positive, optimistic, supportive, enthusiastic, nurturing, fun-loving people and stay away from toxic and negative people and situations. I would seek out adventures and experiences that were life-giving. I would engage in activities that feed my soul. I would pursue my calling with passion. I would be free. My spirit would soar. I would light the dark and heal the world!

This newfound approach to life reminded me of the book *The Polar Express*. Every Christmas, I read that book, even though my kids were grown, and every year, tears would form when I got to the last pages about how the bell has stopped ringing for so many. I was not going to let that happen to me.

In the movie version of the book, the conductor says that it doesn't matter where the train is going, what matters is getting on. I saw it as a great metaphor for life. When we wake up, we get on the train.

And then it's about paying attention to the scenery and not just the destination. It's living more intentionally, more fully, with more awareness. It's about being more present and living in the moment. It's recognizing that God doesn't care so much about what we *do* but rather who we *are*. It's about how we show up in the world that matters most.

I'll give you an example. We have two postal carriers on our block, our regular guy and the guy who fills in for him every so often. They show up completely differently. Our regular guy walks very slowly, with his head down the entire time, staring at the envelopes in his hand, avoiding eye contact at all costs. My kids tell the story of the time they were out playing and one of them fell off his bike. He was lying on the sidewalk wailing when the regular postal carrier came by. And what did the postal carrier do? He walked right around him without even acknowledging his presence.

The postal carrier who fills in looks up, smiles, and is happy to start a conversation with the people on his route. He evens stops to shoot hoops with the kids in the driveway.

We rarely look up! Why is that? Why are we so busy? When did we become so important that the world can't function without our constant, ongoing involvement? We're busy but not productive, chasing life but not finding meaning, inundated with noise yet desperate for peace.

I don't think we have to wait until we die to experience heaven. I believe we can experience heaven here and now. When you open your eyes and begin living with awe, you realize that it's been here all along.

How about you? Are you ready to live life in awe and invite the magic and mystery to become part of your everyday experience? Are you ready to experience heaven right here, right now? When you begin living life as a grand adventure instead of a fearful journey, not only does it change everything in your own life for the better, but that goodness spills out into the lives of those you touch. Does it impact how you give? You bet it does! What if your giving set off a chain reaction that lit up the world? It could happen. But it starts with you and your ability to live life with more awe.

8

Your Magnificence and Your Calling

———————•———————

I am fascinated with near-death experiences (NDEs) and the stories of people who have died and experienced life on the other side. A number of books have been written on the topic, and I have read them all. But my absolute favorite is *Dying to Be Me* by Anita Moorjani.

Anita had Stage 4 cancer and had a near-death experience when her organs shut down. While she was in that state between living and dying, she came to understand what had caused her illness and discovered a profound appreciation for herself. When she returned to consciousness, a miracle happened: she recovered fully in a matter of weeks. In her book, she shares many extraordinary insights, but the most important thing she learned was that we all need to love ourselves and recognize our magnificence.

When was the last time you looked in the mirror and said, "I love you"? When was the last time you exclaimed, "I am magnificent"? If you are like many of us, you might have never said those things to yourself. We don't like to claim our beauty. We're not comfortable admitting that we have unique gifts, talents, and strengths. We worry what others will think of us if we "get too big for our britches," as my grandma used to say. Not only does this keep us living small, it keeps us from sharing the truth of who we are with the world.

Who we are impacts what we do and what we see as our life's work. But if we are living small, we allow ourselves to become enmeshed in the everyday details of life and never look beyond them. Many of us don't know what our life's work is because we've never never taken the time to really explore who we are and just how we might share our gifts, talents, skills, knowledge, wisdom, experiences, hurts, pains, joys, and loves with a world that desperately needs what we have to give.

It's possible that the truth of who we are has gotten buried under piles of laundry and bills, has hidden behind careers that are unfulfilling or marriages that break our hearts, has been covered by the responsibility of caring for children or elderly parents, or has become lost in the reality of a broken world. If so, it's time for you to rediscover yourself. Begin the process of figuring out who you were created to be and how you might live from that place.

There are lots of assessment tools you can use that help identify your personality type, strengths, passions, spiritual gifts, and other aspects of who you are. And those tools can be very helpful as a starting point, but I'm going to suggest that you already know many of the answers. You've lived long enough and had enough life experiences to have a strong sense of who you are at the core.

Carving out quiet time on a regular basis will help you to hear that still, small voice of truth within that remembers the authentic you. Spending time with supportive friends and family can help as well. They often see things in us that we aren't willing to own. As I was struggling to overcome my fears and step out into the bigger world and God's plan for my life, my closest friends and family provided the strength I needed to own my gifts and talents and have the courage to take risks and reach for something more.

At that time, my friend Mary said something so simple and profound that it gave me wings. We were at a meeting discussing a new project. How I might help get it started was part of that discussion, and when Mary described the role she saw that I could play, she said, "That's her gift."

Those words went straight to my core. They were that powerful! To hear someone who had known me for a very long time and with whom I had worked on many projects voice what she saw as my unique gift in the world gave me permission to be and do what she saw in me. I knew what she said was true, but hearing it from her mouth solidified it for me. I could now take what she said and run with it.

But first, I needed to understand how it related to my calling. Did I have a calling? About that same time, my girlfriend and I went to see the theatrical production of *Wicked* together. I had seen it before with my husband, but it wasn't until I saw it with my friend Verily that the power of it really hit me.

The two actresses who played the main characters, Glinda and Elphaba, were exceptionally talented and known in the theater business as a triple threat because they can act, sing, and dance. What I saw were two extraordinary women who were sharing their gifts with the world. And it was clear to me that they were devoting their lives to a calling. They brought it all, night after night, and left it there on the stage for a mesmerized audience to experience, absorb, and take with them on their journey.

I left the theater that evening transformed and swore to myself that I wouldn't die with my song unsung. I began to ask myself if I had ever given all I had to anything. Had I ever put it all out there for the world to see? Had I used all of my gifts, talents, skills, knowledge, and wisdom in pursuit of my calling?

This idea of a calling, a purpose, a mission is not easy to grasp. It takes time, patience, and some digging to figure out why we're here. But we *are* here for a reason—every one of us. We each have a unique calling that God has destined just for us. And if we don't claim it, the world will miss out on the beauty, breath, and soul of our being.

Have you found your calling? Did you know you had one—or perhaps more than one, revealing themselves at different stages of your life? Have you listened to the urges and nudges that keep showing up at the most inconvenient times? Do you find yourself ignoring the messages the universe is sending you because you're too busy with the kids, your career, or the overall messiness of life?

Stop ignoring those urges and nudges. Listen to the voice of your soul that has been calling out to you since you were a little girl, that thing that keeps showing up year after year in subtle and not so subtle ways. Pay attention to the synchronicities and coincidences in life that are trying to get your attention. Remember who you are deep within.

What do you dream about? What did you want to do with your life when you were a little girl? Whose life do you envy? What does your gut tell you to do? What are you passionate about? What gets you jazzed? What voice do you hear in the silence?

All of it, all of the pieces of your life—even the brokenness and pain—are leading you to where God is calling you, to where he needs you out in the world.

Here is the formula, as I once saw it used by Wayne Dyer:

Gifts + Talents + Values + Passions + Experiences = Calling

No one can tell you what your calling is. Only you can determine that for yourself. But I can tell you that when your calling is authentic and aligned with the Divine, it will manifest itself in service to others. It will bring meaning to your life and healing to the world. It may be complicated or simple, grandiose or surprisingly normal, but whatever it is, it's yours. All yours. And the world will be blessed by it.

Whatever your calling is, two things are true for all of us: We are all called to be a light in the dark. And we are all called to heal the world. Let your acts be acts of service because we are all part of something bigger than ourselves. And let your acts be acts of love because each act of love raises the vibrational level of the planet.

Don't keep us waiting any longer. Bring it!

9

Face Your Fears and Shine Your Light

Before I stepped back into the "work world," I was a stay-at-home mom. But as most parents know, that is a misnomer. I was rarely at home. If I wasn't carpooling my children to and from school and activities and play dates, I was volunteering at their schools, at our church, and in our community. I wanted to use my gifts and talents to make things better in the world, so I would identify a situation that I thought could be improved and try to figure out how to do so.

I thought I had the best of intentions and was just being helpful. But as conflicts arose, I sometimes found myself getting angry—at the institutions that were doing it all wrong, at the idiots who couldn't get it right, at the imperfect world itself. It took many years before I realized that the anger I was feeling wasn't all about what was going on out there. The anger was actually inside of me.

That anger within colored how I saw the world and how I interacted with my fellow citizens. It really wasn't the most effective way of being. Everything changed when I finally decided to stop trying to fix things outside myself and turned inward to clear the blockages, resolve the anger, and heal the darkness that had settled in me.

Once I cleared the darkness within, the world outside didn't look so dark anymore. People didn't annoy me as much. Situations didn't seem hopeless. As peace and joy began to well up within, I began to see light in the darkness. And I knew I had to share my newfound perspective because when we clear the blockages within, we can then become a vessel through which God pours his love to be shared with a hurting world.

How did that transformation within me happen? How did I face the darkness and remove the blockages? First, I had to heal the wounds within, many of which were sustained as a result of my father's illness and death from cancer when I was just eighteen years old. In addition to heart-wrenching grief, I had feelings of resentment and guilt all knotted up inside. Once I worked through layers of unresolved emotion, I had to face my fears and regain my willingness to fail. It was scary, but I knew I had the ability to pick myself up, brush myself off, and keep going if I fell down in the process. And I knew I had that ability because I had demonstrated it years earlier when I was in my twenties.

At that time, I was in graduate school at night and working during the day. I had a group presentation that I had been preparing for, but the night before the presentation I was unexpectedly invited to a Cubs game. Never one to pass up an opportunity to spend an evening at Wrigley Field, I chose to go to the game instead of practicing my presentation. I had given many presentations in my life and wasn't concerned in the least.

The next night, my group of four got up to present, and when the first presenter finished, I was up. I stood in front of the class of about twenty with my cue cards and slides and began to speak. But as I was talking, I realized that I really didn't know what I was going to say next. Rather than winging it like I had done many times before, I froze. That would have been bad enough, but despite the fact that my brain had frozen, my mouth was moving, babbling in an incoherent fashion. I heard myself, but I was unable to stop.

The audience was clearly uncomfortable with the disaster they were witnessing. One woman in front kept smiling and nodding encouragingly, hoping I would recover my composure. Others just looked down, perhaps in the belief that I might be able to get through my part of the presentation if no one was paying attention. Even the professor was doing his best not to notice.

I eventually stopped babbling and turned it over to the next presenter. When we finished our presentation and headed back to our seats, a break was announced. I quickly left the building to take a walk and try to calm myself. I wanted to just leave and go home, but I had left all of my things back in the classroom. I would have to go back and face my peers. Somehow I got through it.

Nothing that embarrassing had ever happened to me. I had failed before, but never so publicly. What I learned that day was that I could fail in a big, public way, and it changed everything for me. I began to be afraid. I never wanted to have that experience again, and I was afraid that I might. I didn't understand what had happened, nor did I understand what had brought it on. Only later did I come to see it for what it was: my first panic attack.

I became afraid to speak in public, even in small groups. Then my fear began to carry over to other areas of my life. I became claustrophobic on elevators and in skyscrapers, and I had panic attacks on airplanes. I began planning my life around avoiding situations that might be uncomfortable. My life revolved around my fears.

It was awful, and I knew it had to stop. I finally said to myself, no more! I'm not living like this. I will not let fear keep me from doing something that I want or need to do in life. I realized that to get over my fears, I had to step outside of myself. I had to get over my ego. I had to care less about what others thought of me and more about what I could do for others—even when it was scary. I began to face my fears head-on, did things that scared me, and risked embarrassment.

Failing isn't fun, and we rarely like to talk about our failures. But in truth, we all fail. We all make mistakes. If we could just stop making such a big deal of it, we would realize that our failures lead to our successes. I can assure you that it is so much better to be in the water, flailing around, not knowing how to swim, than it is to be standing on the shore afraid to jump in. If more of us would just admit to our fears and our failures, it would encourage others to do the same. Then no one would be left standing on the shore.

And here's the truth of it: We don't just fail once and we don't just face our fears once. We get those opportunities with some frequency, and if you want to be a light in the darkness, you will let your failures point the route to success, face your fears, and be willing to step into the darkness now and then.

What I learned through my own healing was that if I wanted to make a difference in the world, what I really needed to do was to show up and share my light. Doing that disperses the darkness and empowers those we touch to see their own light, revealing their inner beauty, strength, creativity, and genius.

The good news is that when you face your fears and become a light in the world, you will find that you are not alone on the journey. There are many other bearers of light. You know them. They come from all walks of life, but they're doing exactly what they're meant to do. And you can tell by the glow that surrounds them.

10
Piercing the Dark

One night when my husband and I were in the city having dinner with friends, one of my sons, sixteen at the time, was home alone in our safe, suburban community. His call came as something of a surprise. He wanted us to know that the electric company had just left a message saying that they would be turning off the power for about four hours. As I was talking to him, the power shut down and he was immersed in the dark. And while I had never known him to be afraid of the dark, he was petrified, and his voice began to shake. I called my neighbor, who rushed over to get him and take him to their back porch where the light of their fire pit was blazing and their family was huddled together.

We're all afraid of the dark in some way. Some are afraid of the dark thoughts that creep in as they lie awake at night. Others might be afraid of the darkness spewed out at us and our children through social media, crude song lyrics, and violent video games and movies. And many of us are afraid of the darkness that appears to be engulfing our world in hurt, pain, and suffering.

So what do you do with all this darkness? How do you navigate it? How do you do your part to be light in the darkness without being overcome with fear, grief, and despair? The answer is this: you have to walk toward it and look for the light.

When I was in my twenties, I was a member of Old St. Michael's, a big, beautiful church in the city. The 7:00 p.m. Mass on Sunday night was packed with young adults in their twenties and thirties. The church was alive with energy. I ran the peace and social justice committee, which organized a variety of service projects in our community.

One Sunday morning, I was standing in the back of the church hosting a table for those interested in joining our committee. Before Mass ended, a stereotypical bag lady walked into the church. I immediately hoped that she would not come my way because I didn't know what to say to her. But she came right up to me, looked me in the eye, and politely asked a question. "Where can I leave this donation for the food pantry?" Then she held out a bag full of canned goods. It was a wakeup call.

Around that same time, my husband and I regularly delivered meals prepared by members of our parish to a homeless shelter in the community. We helped serve the meals and then stayed to clean up. It occurred to us that it might be nice to spend a little time with the guests and get to know them better when we were there, so we got a group together to play board games after the meal.

A lot of the people who came to the shelter did not look homeless, they just looked down on their luck. But some seemed to be dealing with more serious issues. One Sunday, a man who appeared to be suffering from mental illness approached the table I was at to ask if he could join us. I could see the concern on the faces of everyone at the table, including the homeless individuals. But there was no way I could say no, so he joined in.

The game we were playing was *Chicago Trivia*. There were questions about the city's history that covered every decade, and except for one man, none of us could answer them. The outcast, the man who looked disheveled and out of sorts, knew every answer. Who was this guy? What had happened to him, and why was he here?

It was another wakeup call.

I could go on and on about all of the times I have seen light in the dark, even if it's just a lightbulb that goes off in my own head when I realize that what I thought was real isn't. Where I thought there was only darkness, there was light. It had just gotten buried, and it just needed someone to see its truth.

What if we need the dark to appreciate the light? What if we need to experience fear, suffering, and sorrow to savor the peace, joy, and love? What if the way out of the darkness is not to run from it but to run to it and find out what it has to teach us? We might not be able to fix every problem, but we can try. We might not be able to stop every injustice, but we can be with people in their suffering.

Everything looks dark until you get up close and take a good look. Sometimes you learn things you never knew about the people you serve, and sometimes you learn things you never knew about yourself. And when that happens, the illumination spreads far beyond that one thing. But before that can happen, you have to open the door and approach the darkness with curiosity and willingness to understand it.

It doesn't help for us to get sucked into the darkness, so how do we step into it without getting lost? We need to be sure our own light is strong. That's why soul-care and self-care are so important for light bearers.

Even when your own light is strong, and even when you are willing to open the door and maybe put one foot into the darkness, you might find yourself pulling back almost immediately. The most natural thing in the world is to avoid pain. The problem is, pain is unavoidable. Pain is a fact of life. And as the Buddhists teach, when we resist whatever is happening in the present moment—including pain—we suffer.

Tonglen is a Buddhist meditation practice that can assist us in countering the human tendency to resist emotional discomfort. Instead of engaging in the habitual response of pushing away pain, the practice of tonglen invites us to bring the discomfort close. It is totally counterintuitive, yet it is a profound way to cultivate inner peace and compassion.

In the simplest terms, the practice is one of taking in and sending out. The practitioner imagines taking in pain and suffering on the in-breath and sending out comfort and compassion on the out-breath. Sending out comfort and compassion is one thing; taking in pain and suffering is another. But what I found as I worked through the practice was that my heart space was large enough to hold the pain and discomfort and, in fact, it's just this enormity of love and light that dissipates the darkness.

In time, we just might find that we're no longer afraid of the dark!

11

Learning to Fly

In my office on the third floor of our home sits a big, green, overstuffed chair. I purchased it when my kids were little. I wanted a comfy place where we could all snuggle and read. When we moved to Chicago, the chair was too big for my bedroom, so we brought it up to the third floor.

At the time, that space was my retreat, the place where I would meditate, journal, and do yoga. It was also the place where I faced my demons, the parts of myself that needed to be healed of grief, anger, guilt, and fear. It's where I ultimately found peace and joy. And it's the place where God called me up and out of my comfort zone.

I didn't want to go. I liked it there. I felt good where I was—good about God, good about myself, and good about my life. My comfort zone was safe, cozy, and easy. And I didn't have to get up and out of my comfort zone, because my husband had a job. He could keep working and take care of us, and I could continue to be a stay-at-home mom. True, my children were growing up and would be leaving home in the not so distant future, so I would not have been able to keep that title forever. But I probably could have faked it for a few more years without anyone knowing.

The truth was, I couldn't kid myself. I knew what I had to do. I had to get up and out of the big, green chair. It was time to trade in the backpack of excuses I had been carrying for a fresh, new set of wings. I couldn't keep the backpack because we all have a weight limit, and if we're carrying too much baggage, we won't be able to fly. And it was time for me to learn how to fly.

I wasn't sure where I was going, but I knew I was being lured out from that place of comfort. You see, we can run from God's dreams for us, but we can't hide. And sometimes we just have to grow into them. That's often what the second half of life is all about. I know this to be true because in my own life, I have heard two callings.

I discovered my first calling after I left the corporate world, determined not to sell my soul for the sake of my career. I then dabbled in some entrepreneurial pursuits, none of which garnered much success or fulfillment. At thirty-one years old, I had my first child. And the minute I saw him, I knew I had found my purpose. For the first time in my life

I knew I was exactly where I was meant to be. So I took a sabbatical from my career—a really long sabbatical—and immersed myself in the world of motherhood.

But there was always a nagging feeling that I had left something undone, that I had not peaked, that I had another purpose in my life.

What I didn't anticipate was that being a stay-at-home mom would have an impact on my self-confidence. I didn't know that when it was time to think about going back out into the "real world," I would have to face fears I didn't even know I had. And the deepest fear of all was that I didn't have what it takes to make my dream come true.

I knew I wanted to own my own business, and I knew I wanted it to be mission-driven. But I had no real role models. No one in my family had ever owned a business. In fact, most of the women in my family had taken the traditional route of staying home and raising kids. So I started looking outside my family to female role models who were succeeding as entrepreneurs. I am forever grateful to a cadre of women—most of whom I've never met—who encouraged me to step outside my comfort zone and follow my dream.

I listened to Dr. Christiane Northrup's radio program, *Flourish*, every Wednesday morning, and I drank in her wisdom and encouragement. I enrolled in Marie Forleo's B-School to learn how to market myself in the age of the internet. I listened to Arianna Huffington talk about how to maintain balance in her Thrive class, and I learned to embrace my feminine power through Claire Zammit's online program. I even attended a small group mentoring program called Raising the Bar, hosted by Jean Houston at her home in Ashland, Oregon. And slowly but surely, my courage increased until I was ready to put it all out there and launch my business.

It's not easy to do the thing we know we need to do. It's not easy to put yourself out there for the world to see and risk failure, criticism, and defeat. But the alternative is unbearable. You absolutely don't want to get to the end of your life and wonder what would have happened if you had just taken a chance and followed your dream.

And here's the other great thing that happens when you're outside your comfort zone: You feel the need for God, all the time. You call on him more and rely on his strength and guidance. And that's always a good thing. That space outside your comfort zone is wide open, sacred space that is unbounded and unfettered. It's where I spend most of my time now. I guess you could say I'm becoming comfortable being uncomfortable.

My time had come. My desire, my dream, and my destiny were calling. The only question that remained was what it would look like.

I wanted to create something that fully expressed who I was and what mattered most to me. It would have to integrate my spirituality, love of entrepreneurship, passion for empowering women and children, and deep desire to serve humanity in a way that had social impact. If it could somehow incorporate my love of wine, that would be an added bonus.

I created AWE Partners from a calling I felt deep within my soul. It became my purpose and my passion. But from the beginning, I knew that it was not about me. I gave it a mission to encourage, inspire, and empower women to make their awe-thentic impact in the world. Starting from a place of soul-stirring, deep purpose, I wanted women to be motivated to share their gifts and talents in service to the universe. I envisioned that as we worked together to direct funding to the most effective organizations addressing our deepest social ills, we would be able to see real change in the beneficiaries of our services, in our communities, and in our world.

Believing that entrepreneurship has the power to not only lift women up but to solve our most challenging social ills, I chose to work closely with heart-centered entrepreneurs who want to align their business mission with their cause-related passion. I saw that it wasn't enough to simply make money as an entrepreneur and keep that corner of life segregated from the larger world and the impact many of us long to have on it. If women could link their entrepreneurship with their passion to give back to the world, real change could happen.

To do that, I also saw that like me, most women needed and even longed to do the self-exploration necessary to rebuild themselves where they were broken, become unstuck, take their self-confidence to the next level, and otherwise take themselves to a place of greater authenticity and self-understanding so their giving could be intentional. When women explore who they are, they ultimately also discover what they have to give and how they want to give it.

But when it comes to making the connection between who they are as entrepreneurs and who they can be as philanthropreneurs, many successful women have remained grounded, like airplanes waiting on a runway for the fog to dissipate. In essence, they just need help dissipating that fog so they can spread their wings and fly. And when that happens, they can help others soar.

Thus far, we've been talking about how to dissipate the fog. Now, let's do a little flying.

12

The Art and Soul of Giving

---•---

Why do we give? Why do we give away our money, time, gifts, and talents? Do we give from a place of guilt or obligation? Do we give because we have so much and many have so little? Do we give from a place of gratitude, in thanks for all of our blessings? Or do we give just because it feels so good—what is often referred to as the warm glow of altruism.

Whatever the reasons, giving is good for us. Studies show that it improves our health by reducing stress and strengthening our immune system. It also improves our self-esteem and enhances overall happiness.

But it's not just why we give that matters, it's what and how we give. There is no set formula. Your giving is as individual as you are. It is unique to you. It springs from your relationship with God or Source and your relationship with yourself. It begins when you recognize your true essence as spirit and your magnificence as a human being. Through self-exploration and spiritual practices, you reclaim your whole, holy self. You are healed and filled, and you can then allow your blessings to overflow into the lives of others and into the world.

In the process of self-exploration, you discover or rediscover your unique gifts and talents, the things you can do better than anyone else on the planet. That includes the ways you express yourself that are like no other because your journey is yours alone. Then you find your purpose in service to humanity by asking what you have been given to share with the world, where you are needed, and how you can help.

Awe-thentic impact is contemplation and action, yin and yang. It's a healthy blending of the true self and the ego, the Sacred Feminine and the Divine Masculine. It's the sweet spot between who you are and what you do. It combines your inner journey to unearth the divine within and your outer journey to care for creation.

Awe-thentic impact is a deeper way of giving. It's a practice that engages the head, the heart, and most importantly, the soul. It leads us out into the world, out beyond our comfort zone. Questions are involved: Who am I? Why am I here? What is my calling? Where do I find meaning? How do I serve? Then it stops asking questions and starts doing—often imperfectly, but always with the best of intentions—leaving the outcomes to God and grace.

What happens when authenticity meets impact? Miracles!

Authenticity + Impact = Miracles

Every form of giving is good when it comes from a place of love. You can't do this wrong!

But you can do this better. And I'll teach you how.

13
Reality Check

The philanthropy arena is overwhelming. I have been involved with nonprofits most of my life as a volunteer, board member, employee, and consultant. I have an MBA with a concentration in the management of nonprofit organizations. I attend classes at the Kellogg Center for Nonprofit Management. I read books and articles, listen to webinars, and attend conferences and networking events. And despite all of this, I am frequently overwhelmed by the size, scope, breadth, and depth of the nonprofit sector.

I can imagine that you may be as well, especially if this is not your chosen area of expertise. You have a life, community, career, family, and friends. You're busy! Add to that the confusion of there being so many worthy causes, a lack of organizational accountability, cases of waste and fraud, and the fact that massive amounts of aid and charitable giving have been unable to solve our most pressing social issues. You are passionate about giving of your time, talent, and treasure, but how in the world are you supposed to find the time to understand and wrap your arms around this whole idea of awe-thentic impact?

I'm here to help. I want to take this vast arena and condense it into the information you need to make smart, effective giving decisions. So let's get started.

First, let's talk jargon. The nonprofit sector can also be called not-for-profit, charitable, tax-exempt, civic, third, independent, voluntary, public interest, and social sectors. Within the arena, there are many kinds of nonprofits. The IRS identifies more than thirty categories of organizations that are exempt from federal income taxes. The most common is classified as a charitable or 501(c)(3) organization. This classification includes public charities, religious organizations, and private foundations.

What separates a charitable organization from other types of tax-exempt organizations is its purpose: it must benefit the broad public interest, not just the interests of its members. The IRS specifies what purposes are permissible. Contributions to these organizations are tax deductible for the donor.

Charitable giving as a percent of disposable income has remained virtually unchanged at approximately two percent over the past forty years according to Giving USA. Yet the number of nonprofit organizations has skyrocketed. In fact, over ninety percent of nonprofits in existence have been created since 1950!

To some extent, the most recent rise in the number of tax-exempt designations granted by the IRS has probably been impacted by the fact that in 2014 the IRS introduced the 1023-EZ, a three-page electronic form that replaced the twenty-six-page application form. Add to that the fact that the IRS has a recent history of approving the vast majority of applications. And once a charity is approved, it is almost impossible for them to have the designation rescinded.

With donations remaining relatively stable while the number of organizations balloons, the not-for-profit community finds itself struggling to attract the funding necessary to carry out its mission. As a result, management is required to spend more time on fundraising than programming, which factors heavily in the high levels of burnout and turnover in the sector.

Even more concerning is the fact that dollars are often being redirected away from the most effective organizations to those that are ineffective and at times outright fraudulent. We need the nonprofit community to perform efficiently and effectively.

So how do we ensure that the more effective nonprofits receive more funding than the less effective? That's where you come in!

14

The Overhead Myth and Impact Measurement

―――――――――・―――――――――

We need to talk. Let me start by asking you to picture one of your favorite products or services. It might be that stunning pair of shoes by Via Spiga, a fabulous Kate Spade bag, or a gorgeous pair of Chanel sunglasses. Maybe it's a spa treatment at your favorite salon or dinner at the hottest new restaurant in town. Perhaps it's a dream vacation at an all-inclusive tropical island resort.

Can you see it? Great.

Now, have you ever asked yourself what the CEO's salary is at the company that provides your favorite products and services? Have you ever wondered about the company's overhead ratio? How often do you question management's approach to running their business? If you're like me, you *never* think about those things. You're simply thrilled that they provide a product or service that you absolutely love, and you willingly spend money to reap the benefits of being their satisfied customer.

So why do we ask these questions of the nonprofit community? Why are we so focused on the salary level of a CEO who runs an organization that is attempting to solve our social ills? Why do we insist that management only spend so much on administrative expenses as they attempt to implement solutions to society's greatest challenges? Why do we not willingly provide the support they need to make a real and sustained impact?

Whenever I ask women how I can help them make more effective decisions with their social impact, nine times out of ten, they tell me they want me to help them identify organizations that spend their dollars on programming rather than overhead.

I get this! I understand that you don't want to see your money wasted. And we absolutely must steer clear of organizations that are guilty of fraud. But when we tell a reputable organization that they can only spend so much on administrative costs, we actually limit their effectiveness. It's been dubbed the "nonprofit starvation cycle" and, thankfully, smart funders are figuring out that this must change if we want to solve the most pressing social issues of our time.

It hasn't helped that Charity Navigator, one of the oldest and most popular charity evaluators, has historically based its rankings largely on the ratio of overhead to programmatic spending. But even they have seen the light after receiving criticism from the nonprofit and funding communities, and they have been working on metrics to assess how well charities measure and report on their impact.

GuideStar is another online service that helps donors evaluate charities by posting information, including the IRS 990 Form for individual nonprofits. GuideStar makes no judgments about the effectiveness of the charities, but organizations can earn Bronze, Silver, or Gold Exchange status depending on how many details about their operations they submit.

GuideStar is also shifting its emphasis from overhead costs to programs and results using its "charting impact" questions that focus on goals and accomplishments. The GuideStar Platinum seal can be earned by charities that display the highest level of transparency by sharing measures of their effectiveness and outcomes.

Charity Navigator, GuideStar, and BBB Wise Giving Alliance have teamed up to dispel what they call the "Overhead Myth" through an ongoing campaign begun in 2013. What are some of the components of this myth? One is that the overhead ratio can be counted on when, in fact, research has shown that the overhead ratio is imprecise and inaccurate. Further, the overhead ratio does not always include compensation, since it is typically counted as a programmatic expense rather than an administrative or fundraising expense. Another component of the myth is that money spent on administration and infrastructure does little to help the organization's clients. But if the organization is performing poorly—or worse, fails—those clients will not be served. In fact, when organizations have robust infrastructures, including skills training as well as technology and financial systems, they are more likely to succeed. And underinvestment in administrative functions has consistently been linked with poor performance.

In 2016, the leaders of twenty-two infrastructure organizations (dedicated to supporting the health of the nonprofit sector) sent a letter to 1,400 foundations across the country to urge them to support nonprofit infrastructure with at least one percent of their grant budgets.

All of these efforts have been undertaken to shift the thinking from exclusive focus on overhead ratios in determining whether or not to donate to a particular organization.

But what should you focus on instead? Impact!

We all want to make a difference in the world. We all want to know that our life has meaning and purpose. So when you step into the world of philanthropy, wouldn't it be nice to know if you're making a difference? Wouldn't it be nice to know that your time, treasure, and/or talent has had an impact?

You can! By taking a more intentional approach to giving, you can get a sense of your impact—not perfectly, perhaps, but enough for you to feel confident that your giving is not wasted and that your generosity is changing lives. This is the intent of impact measurement, which is becoming more and more prevalent in the nonprofit sector. Be forewarned, however, this is an art, not a science, and we're all still figuring out how to do it well.

The process begins with a *theory of change*, which is essentially a statement by the organization that defines how they intend to carry out their mission. It defines the problem they are trying to solve, who they are serving, and what they need to do to achieve their intended result.

A *logic model* then outlines the steps that must be taken for an intervention to succeed. It shows the links between program objectives, activities, and outcomes. A logic model makes clear who will be served, what should be accomplished, and how it will be done. It consists of the following:

- Inputs: What resources (such as money, time, staff, expertise, methods, and facilities) are committed?

- Activities: What are they doing to address the problem?

- Outputs: What is counted, measured, or assessed? That might be products created or delivered, number of people served, or activities and services carried out.

- Outcomes: What ultimate changes are they trying to achieve? These are generally defined in terms of expected changes in knowledge, skills, attitudes, behaviors, conditions, or status. These changes should be measured by the organization, monitored as part of their work, and linked directly to the efforts of the program. They serve as the basis for accountability.

- Indicators: What are the specific, observable, and measurable characteristics, actions, or conditions that demonstrate whether a desired change has happened toward the intended outcome?

- Impact: What results can be directly attributed to the outcomes of a given program or collective of programs as determined by evaluations that are capable of factoring out other explanations for how these results came to be?

As you decide which organizations to support through your philanthropic giving, you want to be sure that an organization has a well thought out theory of change and a logic model to guide them in their ongoing decision making. They should be able to show you how they measure and track what is needed to evaluate programs. This does not need to be complex, nor does it require a fancy IT system. What it requires is a commitment from the leadership team and board to nurture a culture of high performance and continuous improvement so they can be as effective as possible in the areas they serve.

The information gathered through this process is critical for two reasons. First, it permits the organization to measure and monitor the progress they are making toward reaching their goals on an ongoing basis. If they are serious about the work they are undertaking, they will want to capture this information as feedback for their staff to make course corrections as necessary in a timely fashion. This provides a means for ongoing learning and evaluation, which is critical to success. Second, information about their results and impact prove that their theory of change is accurate and that they are on the right track. This is exactly the type of evidence strategic funders like you are looking for when determining where to donate.

If an organization tells you that what they do can't be measured, it's a cop-out. There is always a way to measure results, even if imperfectly.

What can't be measured are the mystery, miracles, and moments of grace that happen anywhere people of goodwill are reaching out to those in need. All work that is done from a place of selflessness and compassion is good work. All giving that comes from a place of gratitude and love is good giving. I'm not in any way suggesting that we remove the compassion, care, and concern that are at the heart of the nonprofit community.

But if you want to be sure you are making a difference, you have to take it a step further. We absolutely cannot and will not make progress on addressing our social ills if we don't know that what we're doing has lasting impact. The mission may sound wonderful, the people may be compassionate and committed, and the work they do may be important. But if it's not effective, if it's not moving the needle, then it's time to assist them in their efforts to improve or look elsewhere for organizations to support.

We can't keep spinning our wheels. We need solutions, and you are part of the solution! Ultimately, your goal is to identify the result you hope to achieve through your giving, locate the organizations that are doing it most effectively, and lend your support through time, talent, and treasure.

This is philanthropy at its best. This is social impact!

15

Effective Altruism

———•———

You work hard for your money, and you don't like to waste it. You're careful about what you spend and how you invest. But are you also careful about where you donate your hard-earned dollars?

Most people aren't. Most take a somewhat haphazard approach to giving. They write checks to organizations that have a good mission or charismatic leader. They donate to charities their friends and family members support. They give to causes they read about or hear advertised on TV that tug at their heartstrings. They respond to the latest disaster or crisis in the news. That's not a bad thing, it's just not the best approach if you really want to make an impact.

If you want to be effective in life, you have to be intentional. If you want to be a good steward of your money, you need to be intentional about what you spend, how you invest, and where you donate. Begin by establishing an annual review process for your philanthropy so you can strategically plan your giving once a year and make small tweaks as necessary.

I advise adopting an investor mindset to philanthropy and creating a portfolio of giving. Your portfolio should be dedicated to causes you are passionate about that are being addressed by the most effective organizations you can find. When deciding where to donate, ask yourself if your approach is one of charity or philanthropy? Charity is typically an emotional response to a need. Philanthropy takes a strategic approach to problem solving with the goal of eliminating the issues that necessitate the need for charity.

As long as donors continue to give based on emotion alone, there is no incentive for the nonprofit community to focus on effectiveness and problem solving. But that's beginning to change as funders become educated and informed. Your impact can be even greater when you not only address needs but also effect change and encourage greater accountability from the nonprofit community. That's what I want for you.

This more intentional approach to philanthropy has many adjectives associated with it: strategic, effective, result-oriented, outcome-oriented. What it means is that before you make a donation, you ask some important questions about what, how, and to whom you want to give. This does not mean you have to become an expert. There are many intelligent, hard-working, energetic, dedicated, compassionate individuals working diligently to solve our most pressing social issues. You just have to understand what issue you want to focus on and then find the organizations that best address it and support their work.

The truth is, you won't always get it right when choosing, but the times that you do will multiply the impact of your giving. It's about the difference you want to make in the world and who you believe has that same conviction and can carry it out effectively. So do your research, and if you can, get out into the field to meet those doing the work. Then make your decision. You will gain more knowledge about the issues and maybe even get some first-hand experience. And you will become a more intentional, impactful giver.

I advise providing unrestricted (not program specific) funding for one year initially. Make your donation and get out of the way. Let the experts do their work. Offer advice and support only if asked. Don't expect them to adjust their strategy or programming based on what you think will work better. If you don't trust them, you shouldn't fund them. It's that simple.

Monitor their progress using the measurements they use. If after the first year you continue to be impressed with the organization, by all means provide additional, longer-term funding and develop a mutually beneficial partnership with them.

In the end, deciding where to fund will come down to doing your homework, trusting your gut, and leaving the outcome to God—kinda like everything else in life.

16

Portfolio of Giving

Your soul-searching and due diligence have paid off! You have identified those organizations you feel called to support. But you're not done just yet. Now you need to make some decisions about what, when, and how to give.

I highly recommend working with your financial advisor, accountant, and/or attorney to make the best decisions for your personal situation.

What to Give

What level of engagement do you want to have? Giving can come in the form of time, talent, and/or treasure.

Time = Volunteer

A great way to get to know an organization is to volunteer. Locate a nonprofit in your area so it's convenient for you to make a commitment. Then ask how you can help. A good organization will welcome your assistance and provide many ways for you to contribute.

Talent = High Engagement

Once you've identified an organization that you believe is effectively addressing a cause you are passionate about, you may decide to become more involved than simply volunteering or giving money. High engagement philanthropists realize that social change requires substantive participation. This may include serving on a board, assisting with fundraising, networking, advocacy, or finding other purposeful ways of sharing your gifts and talents.

Treasure = $ $

A critical way to help an organization you trust is to provide funding that lets them carry out their mission effectively today and plan for the future. That might be in the form of cash, a check, or a credit card. It could also be in the form of appreciated assets such as stocks, bonds, or mutual funds. You might even set up a bequest payable upon your death or name the charity as a beneficiary of a life insurance policy or retirement plan. And instead of cash, you can make an in-kind donation by giving goods and services the organization will then not have to purchase.

You might choose to provide the funds in an unrestricted way, contributing to the organization's general operating budget, allowing them to decide how best to use the funds. Alternatively, you could choose to designate funds for capital improvements to scale up their operations, give them to support the organization's infrastructure, or even designate them for use in outcomes measurement to help them measure the impact they are having. Finally, you'll want to decide whether to provide funding for one year or multiple years.

When to Give

You will also need to decide when to give, particularly if you have a substantial amount of wealth to share. Do you want to give annually or within some other time frame? Do you want to give it all away while you are alive to maintain maximum control, or do you want to set up a foundation to carry on your legacy once you're gone?

How to Give

Aside from giving directly to an organization, there are a variety of giving vehicles to explore with your financial advisor. These include donor-advised funds (DAF), foundations, charitable remainder trusts, and charitable lead trusts.

Discussing Philanthropy with Your Financial Advisor

I'm always amazed to hear from a client that their financial advisor does not discuss philanthropy with them. How can that be? If you're talking about your financial goals, a comprehensive discussion should include how much you spend (budget), invest, and give away. In fact, most high net worth individuals expect to discuss philanthropy with their financial advisor. But it does not always happen. Advisors who are not knowledgeable about the subject of philanthropy may avoid it. Others may not believe that it is their role to address the topic and just focus on their core services. Some financial advisors may be concerned that philanthropy is far too personal a topic for them to discuss with their clients.

If philanthropy is important to you, then shouldn't you be working with a financial advisor who includes it as part of your annual review? Depending on how complicated your financial situation is, you might also want to speak with your tax accountant and/or attorney.

Here are some questions to ask:

- Based on my current financial position, how much do you recommend I give annually?

- Based on my financial projections, how much am I likely to have to pass on or donate at the end of my lifetime?

- How much do you recommend I pass on to my heirs and how much should I donate to charity?

- What tax or estate planning considerations should I be aware of?

- What do you recommend I donate (cash, appreciated assets, personal property, real estate)?

- Should I consider establishing a formal giving vehicle?

- What are the pros and cons of each vehicle?

- If I choose a vehicle, is the decision irrevocable?

- How should I fund the vehicle initially and in the future?

- Which vehicles permit me to donate anonymously?

- Which vehicles permit me to maintain control over my investments and grant decisions?

- Should I give away all of my assets while I'm living or establish a foundation to carry on my legacy and permit my family to retain control?

- How can I include my family in my philanthropic endeavors?

These questions will get the conversation started and allow you to begin exploring how to make wise financial decisions for your philanthropic giving. If you believe that your financial advisor cannot adequately answer your questions or is simply not interested in having this discussion, consider finding a new advisor.

Don't expect your advisor to be knowledgeable about the causes or issues that are important to you or to be able to identify organizations that are addressing these issues. For this, you would be better served by a philanthropy advisor.

Are You a Philanthropist?

What if you don't have a lot to give and don't use a financial advisor? You're just hoping to have enough to get your kids through college and retire before you turn eighty, but you have a heart for giving and are passionate about your cause. Can you still be a philanthropist?

Heck, yes! Anyone can be a philanthropist!

It doesn't matter who you are, what you make, or how much you have in savings. Everyone has something to give. Sometimes we hear about people donating millions and even billions to philanthropy, and we think our small donation means nothing. Does your $25, $100, $1,000, or even $10,000 make a difference? You bet it does! The nonprofit community needs the support of donors at all giving levels, so never think what you give is not enough. It's not about how much you give, it's about why and how you give.

I suggest narrowing your focus of support to three organizations addressing the causes you are most passionate about. That way, you can consolidate your giving and have a greater impact. It costs an organization to process your donation, so a gift of less than $25 is probably not making much of a difference. You will have more impact by making larger donations to fewer organizations.

If you don't have a lot to give monetarily, perhaps you can give of your time and talent. Nonprofits can't operate without a cadre of volunteers. Don't discount the value you bring by sharing yourself.

If you have a desire to give, you are a philanthropist. If you want to share yourself in service to the world, you are a philanthropist. If you want to make an awe-thentic impact, you are a philanthropist. No more wondering if you have something to give. We need you out there!

17
Social Enterprises and Impact Investing

———————•———————

Supporting organizations that are doing good by sharing your time, talent, and treasure isn't the only way to make your awe-thentic impact. You can also make a significant impact through conscious choices about how you spend and invest your money.

Although much attention is paid to the litany of social challenges we face around the globe, we rarely hear about large-scale solutions to our most pressing problems. This has been attributed to declining government funding, lack of impact from corporate social responsibility (CSR) programs, little social innovation from the nonprofit sector, and the inability to scale mission-based solutions. Our historic reliance on government and the nonprofit sector to address our social ills does not work to the degree that we need it to if we want to make progress and find long-term solutions.

With a lack of resources being an ongoing challenge, one approach that nonprofit organizations have attempted with some degree of success is to create a source of earned-income to fund their programming. A simple example is "fee for service" in which a nonprofit charges for the services it offers its beneficiaries. When possible to do so, this is a fabulous way to create an ongoing revenue stream.

A more challenging and risky approach is to launch a social enterprise whose purpose is to change the world for the common good by focusing on business and social goals simultaneously. Social enterprises fall between a traditional nonprofit, which is reliant on philanthropy, and a traditional for-profit, whose purpose is exclusively revenue generation.

As an entrepreneur and philanthropist, I am a huge fan of the social enterprise concept. However, it is important to acknowledge that running a profitable business is never an easy task, especially if resources are already limited. Additionally, if staff members do not have the skill sets required to successfully launch and run a business, additional strain will be put on their already limited resources, and the likelihood of success will be slim.

There are more promising opportunities with for-profit and not-for-profit social enterprises led by entrepreneurs. They are using the methods and disciplines of business and the power of the marketplace to advance their social, environmental, and human justice agendas with the sales of products and services as the primary source(s) of revenue. According to the Social Enterprise Alliance, they are distinguished from other types of businesses, nonprofits, and government agencies by three characteristics:

- The organization directly addresses an intractable social need and serves the common good, either through its products and services or through the number of disadvantaged people it employs.
- Commercial activity is a strong revenue driver.
- The common good is its primary purpose.

Around the globe, there are a multitude of ideas being implemented to address unmet needs in affordable healthcare, safe water, housing, alternative energy, climate change, education, job training, agriculture, finance, and other social issues.

Who doesn't love purchasing from a company with a double bottom line, profit and purpose? Women, in particular, tend to base their buying decisions on how a company's mission aligns with their personal values. But shopping isn't the only way to support these organizations. If the social enterprise is a nonprofit, you can donate directly. Or consider incorporating impact investing into your investment portfolio.

Impact investing is the term used to describe investments made into companies, organizations, and funds that generate a financial return as well as social and environmental impact. The arena includes both for-profit companies that have an explicit intent to have social impact via their business model or practices and nonprofits with revenue and earned income streams.

Originally called socially responsible investing, it was previously limited to screening stocks or industries. For example, when using negative (or avoidance) screening, you chose not to invest in companies whose products or services were considered harmful, such as tobacco, gambling, and pornography. Affirmative screening sought out investments in industries that provided positive benefits such as renewable energy, clean transportation, natural food, and environmentally friendly cleaning products.

Today, socially conscious investors screen their investments using the environmental, social, and governance (ESG) criteria. Environmental criteria includes how a company performs as a steward of the natural environment. Social criteria is comprised of how a company manages relationships with its employees, suppliers, customers, and the communities in which it operates.

Governance deals with a company's leadership, executive pay, audits and internal controls, and shareholder rights.

Historically, a sustainable and responsible investment approach did not provide the same financial returns as a more traditional approach that focused exclusively on profits. But that is changing. Data now shows that investments focused on sustainable, long-term social and environmental impact can provide comparable returns. Consider how willing you are to forego some financial return, if necessary, to ensure your investments are creating positive and measurable social or environmental impact.

Additionally, impact investing opportunities exist across asset classes including cash, fixed income, public and private equities, venture capital, and real assets. So you have options when determining the right mix for your impact investment portfolio. You can also choose between investing into a managed fund or investing directly into companies. This will likely be determined by your sophistication as an investor and how much time you choose to spend in up-front due diligence, monitoring, and involvement with your investee.

Impact investing is still in its infancy, and there are challenges to be overcome. Specifically, it is difficult to accurately measure social impact, and the existing tools for measuring tend to be expensive and time-consuming. Yet progress is being made to standardize impact measures. Impact Reporting and Investment Standards (IRIS), a program of the Global Impact Investing Network, is the catalog of generally accepted performance metrics that leading impact investors use to measure social, environmental, and financial success, as well as to evaluate deals and grow the credibility of the impact investing industry.

Despite the challenges, the potential is exciting. Big name financial players are stepping into the arena, so have a conversation with your financial advisor. It is just one more step toward making your awe-thentic impact!

18
Just Begin

―――――――――――•―――――――――――

Awe-thentic impact begins with you, your true self in all it is becoming, fully alive and fully engaged. You then take yourself out into the world to share your gifts and talents effectively and transform your piece of the planet.

We need you out there. We need you to heal your wounds, slough off the old and birth the new you. We need your truth and your authentic self. We need you to step outside your comfort zone, face your fears, live intentionally, and stop playing small. We need you to step into the darkness and shine your light. In other words, we need you in all your brilliance, magnificence, and power!

The miracle happens as your giving gently returns to you in gratitude from those touched by your generosity. And in receiving, you realize, possibly for the first time, that your life has a deep sense of meaning and purpose.

You are powerful. You are free. You are meant for so much more. There is a greater story being played out, and you are an integral part of it. The world's problems aren't going away easily and they can't be solved by your head alone. You need to engage your head, heart, and soul—the trinity of awe-thentic impact.

Don't assume somebody else is going to take care of it. You are the solution. You are the heroine! Be intentional about what you spend, how you invest, and where you give. Identify solutions to our social ills and support those who are effectively implementing those solutions. Get close to the problems and the people who are suffering, look them in the eye and see yourself reflected back—so you can both heal. Share what you've learned. Share the wisdom. Give them courage. Empower them to recognize that they are the heroine of their own journey.

We're in this together. We need each other. We need to encourage, inspire, and empower each other to become all that we are capable of becoming and to bring to the world the best we have to offer. We need to light the dark and heal the world.

So what will you do now? What do you hear your life calling you to? Do you envision a future of unlimited possibilities for yourself?

This is just the beginning, and you are not alone. There will be so much more to learn, to discover, to experience. Who knows where the path might take you? What are you waiting for?

Just begin!

Appendix A

Tips from the Giving Guru

Effective giving begins with you. Before you start identifying causes, selecting organizations, and sharing your time, talent, and treasure, you need to do some soul-searching. Here are some things to consider and questions to ask yourself before you step out into the world and make your impact.

Get Comfortable Being Authentically You

For many of us, it takes a long time to get to the place where we're finally comfortable showing the world our true self. Sometimes it takes a long time just to figure it out for yourself. As children, we create a façade to protect ourselves from the blows and digs the world sends our way. Although this self-protection may be necessary, it can also prevent you from revealing the depth of your being and living fully true to yourself.

There's work you were made to do that won't get done if the authentic you remains hidden. If you haven't already done so, be honest with yourself and muster the courage to share your beauty with the world.

You can do hard things!

Heal Your Wounds

We're all wounded. That's just the way it is. Nobody gets through life unscathed. But if you carry the wounds with you and define your life by them, you live in bondage, and that's not living! If you aren't at least aware of what your wounds are, you can sometimes cause more harm than good.

Work through your wounds, whatever they are. Get help if you're not sure where to begin. Loving care is available, and you don't have to go it alone.

You are brave!

Nurture Your Soul

To be yourself fully and know why you're here, you need to find stillness and align with Source. It is this time spent in quiet that ignites the flame within and points us in the right direction.

Use whatever spiritual practice you feel comfortable with: prayer, meditation, journaling, spiritual reading, walks in nature, attending worship services, writing poetry, ecstatic dance.

Your soul will thank you!

Take Care of Yourself

It is impossible to be effective out in the world if you are empty on the inside. It is not being selfish to care for yourself. Sometimes guilt creeps in and leads us to give what we don't have, depleting what is necessary for our own physical, emotional, and spiritual survival. We then become ineffective for ourselves, our families, and others.

Fill your cup so you have something to share. Get a good night's sleep, eat healthily, and exercise. Spend time with loved ones, enjoy hobbies, take a bath, and do whatever else it is that brings you joy and makes you feel refreshed and whole so you can be at your best.

Love yourself!

Design Your Life

When was the last time you sat back and really thought about where you are and where you're headed? Did you know that you can actually design the life of your dreams? It's true!

You can begin right now. Take out a piece of paper and set up columns for all of the facets of your life: spiritual, family, friends, community, career, financial, health, and fun. Start keeping a list of all the things you'd like to see happen in each of these categories and what steps you can take to get there. Just the act of writing it down begins the process of making your dreams come true. Commit to taking one new action each week toward one of your goals. Once you get used to doing this, the momentum will propel you forward. Before you know it, you will start to see real change, and the life of your dreams will slowly become reality.

Dream big!

Invite in Peace, Joy, and Abundance

Have you been living a life of scarcity, believing that there's not enough love, health, money, or adventure to go around? Well, there is! Often, all it takes is a shift in your thinking to realize it.

What is it you want more of? Peace? Joy? Abundance? Love? Meaning? Fulfillment? Invite what you want more of into your life and be open to receiving it. God wants to shower you with abundance in all areas of your life. The more you have, the more you have to share.

Claim it!

Own Your Magnificence

You are amazing! You have unique gifts and talents that no one else in the world has. You have skills, knowledge, wisdom, experience, hurts, joys, pains, and loves. There is no one else exactly like you.

That's why you must own your magnificence and share it with the world. If you don't, we all miss out on what you have to bring us. Don't worry. It's not egotistical when it comes from your soul and is used to bless yourself and others.

Bring it!

Embrace Your Calling

You are here for a reason. You are not a mistake. Your life has meaning and purpose, and it's time to own it.

What are you passionate about? What inspires you? What lights you up and makes you come alive? What brings you joy? How can you take all of who you are and share it in service to the world? We need you.

Shine your light!

Appendix B

To Give or Not to Give

You work hard for your money, and you don't like to waste it. You're careful about what you spend and how you invest, but are you also careful about where you donate your hard-earned dollars?

I advise adopting an investor mindset and creating a portfolio of giving. The awe-thentic process for vetting organizations is designed to be personal, in-depth, and strategic. It takes time and effort to make impactful giving decisions.

Okay to Give

The majority of your giving should be to causes and organizations that you are passionate about, have thoroughly vetted, and make the greatest impact possible. But it is okay to donate a percentage of your overall giving portfolio in the following ways.

Place of Worship

If you have a place of worship that you attend on a regular basis and feel a connection to, you might want to donate a portion of your giving to that organization. It's wise to take a look at that organization's financial statements just to get a sense of their overall health and learn who holds the purse strings. Yes, instances of embezzlement, fraud, and misappropriation of funds do occur in religious institutions, but if you do a little investigation and analysis before you donate, you will make a more educated decision. This is a very personal kind of giving, and you want to be able to feel good about supporting the mission of your faith community.

Alma Mater

Many people feel a connection to the colleges and universities they've attended. Often, there is a sense of gratitude for receiving the knowledge and lessons necessary to be successful in life. And to many, education is considered the foundation of a healthy society. For all of these reasons, the desire to donate a portion of your charitable dollars to your alma mater is understandable.

That being said, the reality is that many educational institutions are the beneficiaries of extremely large endowments.

This means that your donation will not have the same level of impact that it would with other organizations in your giving portfolio. If you have questions, contact the development office at your alma mater to learn more about how your donation will be used. Once again, this is a personal decision and something you'll want to consider in your overall giving plan.

Charities Supported by Family and Friends

If you are philanthropically inclined, chances are your friends and family are as well. Therefore, you're likely to be invited to attend fundraising events and/or provide support for their favorite charities. This can be a good way to learn about worthy causes and organizations. You may want to set aside a portion of your overall giving each year to support the charities supported by family and friends.

Neighborhood Schools and Clubs

If you have kids in your neighborhood, you probably get hit up regularly for donations to their schools, sports teams, and clubs. You should set aside funds to be donated in this way. Not only does it support your local community, it also teaches a kid that courage and hard work are rewarded.

Beggar on the Street

This may not be an obvious one because many advisors, including myself, believe that it is better to give to organizations that provide services for those in need than to give directly to those begging on the street not knowing how the money will be used.

I love the story about two guys going out for a night on the town who pass a homeless man begging. One of them gives the beggar twenty dollars.

"You shouldn't do that. He's just going to spend it on alcohol," his friend says.

"Well, that's what we're going to spend it on," he points out.

The point is, it's probably not the smartest decision to give money to someone begging on the street. But the reality is that there will be times when you pass a person in need, your eyes meet or your heart is touched, and you just feel compelled to give. Go ahead and do it. You have no idea what the impact will be or who might be inspired by your action. I can tell you that I believe my path to philanthropy began on the steps of St. Peter's Church in Chicago where my dad always gave a dollar to a beggar.

Always leave room for what I call the mystery, miracles, and moments of grace that result from your giving. Just do your best, and leave the outcome to God.

Not Okay to Give

Sometimes it is just not a good idea to give because you are being caught off guard, may not know that the organization is legitimate, or have not had an opportunity to research the group. Below are a few circumstances under which you should not donate.

Door-to-Door Solicitation

Not only can it be dangerous to open your door to a stranger, it can also result in a waste of your time and money. When you're face-to-face with someone who is making an appeal for help, it can be very difficult to think strategically about how this fits into your overall giving plan. The reality is that it's hard to say no to someone who is passionate about their cause when they're standing at your door. So don't put yourself in this position. You can post a "No Soliciting" sign or simply choose to not answer the door. Consider using the same approach with charitable organizations soliciting on the street. Just keep walking.

Over the Phone

Phone solicitation can occur at all hours of the day or night. Numbers are typically dialed at random via computer. If you answer the call and there is a live person on the other end, they may or may not actually work for the organization they are promoting. Often, they are employed by a fundraising company and are paid a percentage (which can be quite large) of your donation. No matter how knowledgeable they sound or how desperate their plea, you should never agree to donate over the phone. And never provide your credit card information. Get caller ID through your phone service provider and don't answer calls from numbers you don't recognize. If you do end up on the phone with a fundraiser, politely ask them to place you on their "do not call" list or simply hang up.

Mail Solicitation

If you have made charitable donations in the past, it's likely that you receive a host of solicitations by mail. These can arrive from organizations to whom you have already given money, those you have at least heard of, and those with which you are unfamiliar. This form of solicitation is easier to manage because there is no live person at your door or on the phone. Make a strategic decision about whether or not to give. Here's the approach I suggest:

- If the organization is one in which you have no interest, throw it away.

- If the organization interests you but you have never donated to them, add them to your file of organizations to be vetted. You can research them more thoroughly during your annual review process.

- If you have donated to the organization previously and would like to continue supporting them, take a look at the request to determine if you want to make an additional donation. But I suggest making your giving decisions once a year during your annual review process so you don't continue to spend time stewing over how often and how much to donate.

- Finally, never decide to give to an organization just because they sent you a "gift" in the mail. You have probably received boatloads of coins, mailing labels, religious medals, and other items from a variety of nonprofit organizations. Wouldn't you prefer to see their funding used to further their cause? Keep the gift if you like, but throw the solicitation in the trash.

Television Ads

This is another form of solicitation that can be very hard for compassionate people to ignore. Pictures of sick children, starving refugees, wounded veterans, abused animals, and others who need help are gut-wrenching. They're meant to tug at your heartstrings and they do. But making a decision to donate to an organization just because their video clips are compelling is not smart giving.

Although many of the organizations that advertise in this way are worthy of your philanthropic dollars, some are not. It's up to you to make that determination before you give. So if you see a cause or an organization that touches you deeply, make a note of it and add it to your list of organizations to be vetted during your annual review process.

Immediately Following a Natural Disaster

I know that everyone won't agree with me here, but I don't recommend giving immediately following a natural disaster because that's exactly the time when money is donated at a rapid pace and in great quantities from around the world. Aid agencies are frequently ill equipped to handle the influx efficiently. As a result, much of it is wasted.

Additionally, natural disasters trigger the appearance of fake agencies that will gladly take your money with promises to help those in need. Sadly, the money never gets to the intended victims. What I suggest is waiting for a couple of weeks following a disaster until the initial mayhem has subsided. Then, if you still feel called to help, you will have had time to do some research and determine which agencies are providing the most effective services.

Appendix C

Causes and Issues

- Animal Welfare
- Arts & Humanities
- Capital Punishment/Death Penalty
- Children
- Community Development
- Disaster Relief
- Diversity & Equality
- Domestic Violence
- Education
- Employment/Job Training
- Environment/Climate Change
- Family
- Gun Control
- Health & Disease
- Health Care Reform
- Homelessness
- Human Services

- Human Trafficking
- Hunger
- Immigration
- International Issues
- Mental Health
- Natural Disasters
- Pornography
- Poverty
- Racism
- Religion
- Research
- Safety & Security
- Terrorism
- Veterans Affairs
- Violence
- Women's Issues

Appendix D

The Awe-thentic Approach to Identifying Effective Organizations

What does a well-run nonprofit or social enterprise look like? The awe-thentic approach to identifying effective organizations focuses on six major areas.

Leadership/Talent

The number one thing to consider when choosing an organization to support is the management team and board of directors.

Start with the executive director (ED) or chief executive officer (CEO).

- Is she a visionary?
- Is her leadership style collaborative, and is she committed to the team, the organization, and the cause?
- Does she have demonstrated success in this or related areas?

- Does she surround herself with talented, self-disciplined, self-motivated managers and staff?
- Is her salary tied to performance?

Next, look at the rest of the organization.
- How long has the management team been in place?
- Are salaries at a level to attract and retain talent?
- Are education and training provided to the team members?
- Is a culture of learning encouraged?
- What is the makeup of the board of directors?
- Is the board engaged, and do they provide resources, support, and coaching to the team?
- Is the organization transparent?

Financials/Accountability

Take a rigorous look at the financials and how the organization holds itself financially accountable.
- How long has the organization been in existence?
- What is their revenue size?
- Do they have audited financial statements and internal checks and balances?
- Do they have a sustainable funding model?
- Do they have the financial wherewithal to scale their operations?

- What are their important financial ratios?
- Do they have an endowment and/or operating reserves at least equal to the annual budget?
- Are they cost effective in achieving social benefits?
- How will new funding be allocated?

Mission

The management team may be great and the financials in order, but if the mission is inadequate or does not fit with the causes you want to support, then it may not be a suitable charitable organization for your giving. Scrutinize the mission.

- Is their mission statement clearly articulated?
- What social challenge are they working to address? Is it among the causes you want to support or related to them?
- Are they addressing a critical need?
- What is their theory of change (the causal chain that links interventions to goals)?
- What is their logic model (set of steps to achieve goals)?
- Are they aware of best practices in the sector to understand what is possible and gather new ideas on how to improve?
- Are they strategic in their thinking?

- Are they flexible and does their strategy adapt to a changing reality?
- Are they innovative?
- Do they take calculated risks?

Programming

The nonprofit's mission needs to be reflected in programming that addresses that mission. Look at the organization's programs.

- What are they trying to accomplish?
- What programming do they offer?
- Do they have clearly defined goals?
- Are they using evidence-based strategies to achieve their goals?
- Is their programming unique and transformative?
- Do they design their programming based on conversations with the beneficiaries of their services?

Outcomes Measurement

This is, in large measure, where the rubber meets the road. You want to know that what the organization envisions and implements actually works. Examine that.

- Is there a body of evidence to prove that their programming works?

- How do they know?
- Do they use technology (dashboards) to track progress?
- What metrics do they use to measure and monitor progress for continuous improvement?
- What are the key indicators of success?
- Do they know how many people benefit from their programming and by how much?
- Are they in close contact with their constituencies and stakeholders (clients, donors, volunteers, partners) to solicit ongoing feedback on a real-time basis to evaluate and improve mission effectiveness?
- Are they committed to quality improvement and is there a process in place to make coarse corrections based on feedback?
- Do they have independently audited or peer-reviewed randomized controlled evaluations of their programming?
- Do they assess impact? That is, do they assess whether the outcomes are the result of their programming versus what would have occurred anyway?
- Do they acknowledge and learn from failures?

Collective Impact

Great nonprofits collaborate with others to maximize impact, share information and ideas, and avoid duplication of services. How and to what end do they collaborate?

- Are they working with other organizations (nonprofits, government, businesses, the public) across sectors to address the issues to achieve widespread impact?
- Are they skilled collaborators?
- Are they more concerned with making an impact than taking credit for their own achievements?
- Do they inspire their following to become involved in their cause?
- Are they involved in advocacy work surrounding their stated mission?

Appendix E

Gutsy Guidebook

Consider this a guidebook to help inspire your Portfolio of Giving (see Appendix F). Two things are needed to make your awe-thentic impact in the world: inner work, which will deepen your knowledge of yourself and will put you in right relation with the beauty and inherent value within you; outer work, which will move you from that in-depth understanding of who you are to how you can enact it in your philanthropic giving.

I have provided questions and thoughts that relate to each chapter of this book. Work through them at your own pace. You don't have to answer every question, just those that resonate with your life experiences.

I suggest establishing a time each year for an annual review of giving. It's best to do it early in the year, and it should coincide with a financial review with your wealth advisor, accountant, and/or attorney. There's no need to go through the entire guidebook each year, though you may find reviewing some of the questions helpful. You will simply need to look at where you are directing your donations and determine if any changes are warranted.

Keep a file labeled "Organizations to Be Vetted." As you come across organizations that interest you throughout the year, make a note and put it in the file. It will save you a lot of time to review these just once a year during your annual review of giving rather than researching organizations all year long.

Once you have worked through the questions, you will be well on your way to making your awe-thentic impact in the world!

1: Happy and Human
- What life experiences have shaped who you are today?
- What might have been helpful to you growing up that you did not have? (This might lead you to a cause or organization you would like to support.)
- What wound, sin, failure, excuse, regret, or fear are you hanging on to?
- Why won't you let it go?
- Can you forgive yourself for past mistakes and failures?

- Can you forgive others who have hurt you?

If you have been struggling to move beyond a wound, failure, or fear and you just can't seem to make any progress, have you reached out to a licensed counselor and asked for help? You are not alone, and it's time, dear sister, to work through it and let it go!

2: Where Are You Stuck?
- What is missing in your life?
- What gets in your way?
- Are you stuck in external places like your marriage, career, or where you live?
- Are you stuck doing something that you're not proud of and just can't seem to stop?
- Do you live with excessive guilt, shame, anger, resentment, fear, worry, or anxiety?
- What things do you use to fill up the emptiness you feel?
- Do you feel a sense of restlessness and, if so, where does it come from?

Write a letter you will *not* send to someone who has hurt you or you have hurt. Just start writing. Don't think about what you're going to say, just let it spill out onto the page. If tears come, let them fall. Write until you get it all out and there is nothing left to say. Then put the letter away where no one will see it and sit with it for a while—a day, a week, a month, a year. See how it makes you feel.

- Has it helped you to let go of some things you've kept deep inside for too long?
- Are you able to forgive the other person or yourself?
- Can you begin to release whatever it is that you're holding on to?

When you're ready, find a way to get rid of the letter that helps to bring closure. Burn it, shred it, or tear it apart. Then let go of it and see if you have another letter inside you just waiting to be written and not sent.

3: You are Good Enough

- Where do you feel a sense of lack in your life?
- Where do you find a need for control, security, or approval?
- Where do you feel resistance?
- Do you have an inner glass ceiling?
- If so, what is etched in the glass?
- How might you shatter the glass ceiling once and for all?
- What helps you know you're good enough?

Take out a piece of paper and begin writing all of the things that you love about yourself, things that make you worthy of taking up space on this planet, things that give you the right to have a voice in the world. Keep writing. This should be a very long list because you are good enough, dear sister!

4: Make Space for Grace

- Where are you between chapters in your life?
- Is there something ending or that needs to end in your life?
- Is something new beginning?
- What might this in-between time teach you?
- How does uncertainty make you feel?
- Do you prefer to always be in control?
- Do you feel your feelings all the way through, or do you have a tendency to rush past them or bury them?

Take out a sheet of paper and draw a vertical line down the center. At the top of the left side, write *Things that Need to End*, and at the top of the right side, write *Things I Hope to Begin*. Then make a list of all the things that fit into each category. Be honest with yourself. Once you have finished, think about what actions you can take to encourage the endings and beginnings that need to happen in your life.

5: Nurture Your Soul

- What is your reason for getting up in the morning?
- What kind of journey are you on: head, heart, soul, or all of these?
- What makes life good, meaningful, and worthwhile?
- What brings you joy?
- Where do you find your deepest satisfaction in life?
- Do you have a daily spiritual practice?
- What voice do you hear in the silence?

If God wrote your to-do list, what would it say? Go ahead, make a to-do list for the next year and include all the things you think God wants you to do (and be).

6: Take Care of You

- How would you describe yourself? (Try to think beyond your roles in life and personality traits.)
- Do you love who you are today?
- What type of person would you like to become?
- What do you do to take care of yourself?
- Who else do you care for?
- What are the things you believe you have to do, should do, and want to do in your life? What would happen if you got rid of the things you believe you should do?

- What could you realistically stop doing for someone else that would change your life for the better?

If you had a whole day to yourself and weren't allowed to do anything for anyone but yourself, how would you spend the day? Make a date with yourself. Find a day on the calendar in the next couple of months that you can take all to yourself. Plan to do your favorite things all day long. If you can swing it, make it a whole weekend!

7: Live Life with More Awe
- Have all your dreams come true? If not, what do you still dream of?
- If there is something you have always wanted to do in life, why haven't you?
- Have you been the author of your life story, or have others written your story for you? If you feel that others have written your story for you, who are they and why have you let them?
- Is there a theme that connects all of your life experiences?
- What would make life magical for you?
- What lights you up and makes you come alive?
- What energizes and inspires you?
- How do you express your creativity?

Set an alarm on your phone for the same time each day. When the alarm goes off, stop what you're doing and take a deep breath. Say to yourself, "Slow down." Then look up and take it all in, wherever you happen to be.

8: Your Magnificence and Your Calling

- What busywork is keeping you from your life's work?
- Have you identified your personal calling or mission in life?
- What unique gifts and talents have you been given?
- What comes easily and naturally to you?
- Where do your natural talents and skills meet your passions?
- Whose life do you envy?
- What do you want out of life?

Plan some time to get away from your daily responsibilities. Get out of your normal surroundings and find a place in nature to just chill. While you're there, ask yourself what life is calling you to. Then take time to listen to the answer. What does your gut tell you to do? You may have to do this more than once—maybe a lot, in fact—before it becomes clear. Trust me, though, it will become clear!

9: Face Your Fears and Shine Your Light

- When was the last time you experienced an epic failure and how did you handle it?
- Did you tell anyone about it? How did they respond?
- Did that failure keep you from going back out and trying again, or did you overcome that failure?
- When you step out into the world, do you find yourself coming up against the same resistances over and over again?
- What are those recurring resistances, and how might you overcome them?
- Who are the light bearers in your life?

If you're comfortable failing at what you attempt and recognize that failure is just one step toward success, then rock on with your bad self. If you're afraid to fail, then it's time to get over it. Spend some time reliving that big failure in your life that keeps you playing small. Analyze it from the safe space you're in now. Ask yourself if it was really such a big deal. Did it really have such a negative impact on your life? Are you ready to move on from it? Think about what steps you can begin to take to move through the failure, learn from it, and take your next steps toward success. It's time!

10: Piercing the Dark

- Are you troubled by the chaos and darkness in the world?
- Can you see light amidst all the pain and suffering in the world? Where?
- How do you find peace amidst the world's turmoil?
- Are you afraid of what might happen if you step outside yourself to help someone in need?
- What experiences have taught you that things aren't always as they seem at first glance?
- What have you learned about yourself by facing the darkness in your own life or the darkness in someone else's life?
- How have you seen love and compassion pierce the dark?

Find an evening when you can be completely alone in your house at night. Find a comfortable place to sit and bring a blanket or other comfort items to your space. Turn off all the lights. Power down all the electronics. Quiet all the noise. Sit there for as long as you can. Just stay there in the dark and see if you can experience peace. Can you sense the light that is always present in the darkness?

11: Learning to Fly
- What urges or nudges just won't go away?
- What fear does that bring up in you?
- How would it feel to step outside your comfort zone?
- Would you be willing to stay there?
- If you could do anything in life and you were guaranteed not to fail, what would you do?
- If money were no object, what would you accomplish?

I'm going to challenge you to begin facing your fears. I know it's scary. Believe me, I have been there. But as hard as it is to face your fears, it's harder to live in fear. So here we go.

Write down everything you're afraid of. Now put them in order from the thing that's least scary to the thing that is most scary. Some of the things you can't do anything about. You're afraid of them, but they might never happen. With the fears you can do something about, begin to face them right now. Take them one at a time. Take however long you need, but start. Here's what's going to happen: You're going to face one fear and realize it wasn't as bad as you thought. And then you'll face the next fear and discover the same thing. And before you know it, you won't be so afraid. And when that happens, you will taste the sweet freedom of life in a new way. Less fear and more courage equals freedom!

12: The Art and Soul of Giving

- To what people and places do you feel a sense of gratitude?
- What are some of your earliest memories of giving and volunteering?
- Who have been some of your philanthropic heroes and role models in life?
- How does the influence of parents, grandparents, or other relatives impact your giving?
- What core values do you want to pass along to your family and friends?
- What role might your family play in your journey as a philanthropist?

Spend some quiet time thinking about how you can best serve and make an impact in the world. Listen for the answers. Then talk with your family (grandparents, parents, spouse, children) about philanthropy and the role you would like it to play in your family.

13: Reality Check
- Why do you give of your time, talent, and treasure?
- What have been your personal experiences as a donor?
- What do you find most fulfilling about giving?
- What is your deepest intention in pursuing philanthropy?
- What kind of legacy do you want to leave?
- How can you share your gifts, talents, and passions with the world?

Begin thinking of yourself as a philanthropist. Consider how you might become more intentional and strategic in your approach toward philanthropy. The most effective philanthropy doesn't just happen here and there. It becomes a way of life. What might this mean for you?

14: The Overhead Myth and Impact Measurement
- What keeps you up at night? What breaks your heart?
- What causes are near and dear to your heart?
- What is the scope of the problem(s) you hope to address?
- What are the root causes of these problems?

- What goals/outcomes/solutions do you seek?
- What evidence-based strategies exist for achieving them?
- What are the chances for success, and how will you measure success?
- Are the problems already being addressed and possibly overfunded?
- What do you want to achieve through your donation?
- Do you want to provide unrestricted or program-specific funding?
- What is your time horizon? Are you investing for the short or long term?

Go through the list of causes and issues in Appendix C. Begin by circling all of those you care about. If you're like me, it's probably most of them. Now narrow that list to the top ten causes/issues you really care about and about which you want to learn more. Finally, narrow the list to the top three causes/issues that you want to get involved with and for which you want to make an impact. This can be a very difficult exercise, but to be effective, you must narrow your focus and trust that others will address the issues that you don't. We're all in this together!

15: Effective Altruism

- How many organizations do you want to develop relationship with?
- How will you identify the organizations that are having the greatest impact on the causes you care about?
- Is it most effective to address the issue at the local, national, or international level, or through a combination of these?
- Is there a group of organizations addressing different aspects of the issue that you can support?
- What is your risk tolerance? Would you prefer to give to a well-established organization that has proven outcomes, or are you comfortable taking a chance on a new organization or approach that does not yet have a track record?
- How will you reach out to the organizations with which you want to develop a relationship?

Appendix D is a comprehensive list of what you should look for when vetting organizations. You don't have to answer every question, but you do want to consider each of the areas outlined and obtain as much information as possible before providing support to an organization.

16: Portfolio of Giving

- What level of engagement do you want to have with the organizations you support, and how much time do you want to devote to philanthropy?
- Do you want to share your time, talent, treasure, or a combination of these?
- How much of your wealth do you want to set aside for philanthropy?
- Do you want to give it all away while you're alive to maintain maximum control?
- Are there charitable giving vehicles you'd like to explore, such as donor advised funds, foundations, bequests, charitable lead trusts, or charitable remainder trusts?
- Do you want to consider making an investment (equity or loan) as a tool to achieve change?
- What profile would you like to have with your giving? Would you like to remain anonymous or publicize your giving in hopes of encouraging others to give?

Be sure to speak with your financial advisor, accountant, and/or attorney to discuss the specifics of your philanthropic giving.

17: Social Enterprises and Impact Investing

- Do you consciously purchase goods and services from social enterprises?
- Have you engaged in socially responsible investing to screen companies in your investment portfolio?
- Do you use ESG (environmental, social, governance) criteria when selecting investments?
- Have you explored impact investing with your financial advisor?

Ask your financial advisor, accountant, and/or attorney if they are knowledgeable about impact investing. If the answer is no, ask around to see if you can identify someone with whom to have this conversation.

18: Just Begin

- Who are you authentically?
- What impact do you want to have?
- What do you hear your life calling you to?
- Do you envision a future of unlimited possibilities for yourself?
- What will you do now?
- What are you waiting for?

We need you out there! Let's get giving!

Appendix F

Portfolio of Giving

Name:
Date:
Core Values:

Personal/Family Mission Statement:

Gifts/Talents/Skills/Knowledge to Share:

Cause/Issue to Address:

> What is the scope of the problem?
>
> What are the root causes?
>
> What goals/outcomes/solutions are you seeking?
>
> What are you funding?
>
> What is your time horizon for addressing this issue?
>
> How will you assess progress/outcomes?

Organizations to Support:

> What are the most effective organizations addressing this issue?
>
> Will you focus at the local, national, or international level?
>
> Are there organizations that are collaborating/engaged in collective impact?
>
> Who are your contact people within the organizations?

Level of Engagement:

> What level of engagement do you want to have?
>
> Will you contribute time/volunteer?
>
> Will you share your talent/engagement and in what ways?

Donations:
> Will you donate money and, if so, in what form?
> Will you provide in-kind support?
> Will the funding you provide be unrestricted or program specific?
> Will you donate annually or make a multiple year donation?
> Will you use a giving vehicle and, if so, which one?

**You will want to complete the above form for each of the causes and organizations you support. To download a free copy of the Portfolio of Giving worksheet, go to https://awepartners.com/portfolio-of-giving.

Acknowledgments

———•———

I have a note I keep at my desk to remind myself of why I'm doing this work on those days when fear and overwhelm get in the way of inspiration and creativity. Here's what it says:

> For all the women in my family who have come before me, especially my grandmothers, great-grandmothers, aunts, and great-aunts. You didn't get to write your own story or live the life of your dreams. Because of you and your sacrifices, I and so many others can. I honor you!
>
> For all the women and children around the world who are suffering, unable to express the truth of who you are, share your unique gifts and talents, and live out your destiny. I pray for you!
>
> For the next generation of light bearers and leaders and seven generations hence, that you will honor and build on the work we have begun to merge heaven and earth for all who inhabit our planet. I bless you!

To my editor, Melanie Mulhall, who took a chance on me and encouraged me with the words, "I think you might be on to something," thank you. You took my voice and words and made them sparkle and shared your insights willingly. You are a genius!

To my designers, NZ Graphics and Step Brightly, your artistry brought life to my words. You are brilliant!

Thank you, Fr. Ken Sedlak, my spiritual director who has challenged me to expand my definition of religion and spirituality for the past three decades. I can't imagine where I'd be if I hadn't joined your spiritual discussion group. I am eternally grateful!

I want to thank my children, family, and friends, who patiently stood by and watched as I reinvented myself midway through life, leaving the cocoon to test my wings. As I grew, you grew with me, even when it meant that who I had been for you in the past would have to change too. Thank you for not holding me back and trusting that our relationship would only grow stronger as I did. I love you!

To my mom, who has shown me that life just keeps getting better and that we can experience heaven on earth, thank you. I am in awe!

Finally, thank you, Jack, my soul mate and partner in life. You always believed that I had made a sacrifice by putting my career on hold to raise our boys. I always believed it was an incredible blessing to be given that privilege. From that first night at the Pump Room, when I wrote my dream on a napkin, and through all of life's ups and downs, you never threw away the napkin or the dream. You have created a space where I can connect with my soul's desire, nurture my gifts and talents, and shine my light in the darkness so that women the world over can do the same. I'm your biggest fan!

About the Author

---•---

Despite studying business and finance in college, Elisabeth Williams realized early on that she was not a good match for the corporate world. The fact that her dad always told her, "You don't need to kiss anybody's ass," probably didn't help. An entrepreneur at heart, she was always drawn to the nonprofit world and is committed to bringing business acumen to the challenge of solving our social ills.

Lis is passionate about guiding women to give, invest, and shop for impact from a place of authenticity. Her firm, AWE Partners, works with entrepreneurs to align their business mission and cause-related passion. She believes that by driving funding to the most effective organizations in the social impact space, we can move the needle on the issues that prevent individuals from living fully and realizing their destiny.

Lis is particularly focused on the empowerment of women and children worldwide. She lives with her husband and two sons in the suburbs of Chicago.

Learn more at www.AWEPartners.com.